To Love and To Be Loved

Establishing Healthy Relationships

Lisa L. Schwarz

Contact the author: Lisa Schwarz
www.Lisa-Schwarz.com
www.Crazy8Ministries.com

Dedication

I would like to dedicate this book to all the residents that have gone through our housing program. Working with them over the years has taught me so much about how relationships profoundly affect who we are and the way we live our lives. I have learned that at the core of most challenges is the desire to love and to be loved and the inability to understand how to connect with God, ourselves, and with others without forfeiting our God-design.

Watching the residents learn about their God-design and teaching them how to guard that design has greatly impacted me personally in my own understanding of God's plan for relationships. It has changed the way I approach those whom I counsel and coach and has helped to define the root of many issues.

Because of this discovery, my own relationships have gone through some sifting over the years as well. I, too, have learned to enforce His most excellent design. While this has improved many of my relationships, a few have been shattered. However, in both cases, I have found true freedom and am experiencing deeper, more vulnerable and transparent connections as a result.

Among these relationships is with my husband, Brad, who has partnered with me to fight for God's design within our marriage. It has been amazing to discover TOGETHER the power we have to redefine the personality of our marriage...even after 25 years! Thank you, Brad, for your partnership in chasing down HIS best for us and for helping me discover what it means to love and to be loved.

I would be remiss if I didn't also mention my daughter Morgan and her friend Vittoria who have followed along as I wrote this book. They were with me when I wrote the very first chapter and read every word of it the minute it was done. With much excitement, they supported me in capturing the concept of healthy relationships, knowing how vital it is to loving and being loved. Thank you, girls, for your support and input! On a lighter note, they were hoping to "get a mention." LOL!

Table of Contents

Prayer Practice

Throughout my years of ministering, counseling, and discipling, I have discovered that many people don't understand how to declare God's Truths into their lives through prayer. We know what it means to ask God for things and to supplicate, but we struggle when it comes to standing firmly on His biblical promises and principles. I've spent many years trying to tell people what it meant, but over the past five years, I have found it more effective to simply demonstrate it.

When the disciples asked Jesus to teach them how to pray, He responded by demonstrating.

> "One day Jesus was praying in a certain place. When he finished, one of his disciples said to him, "Lord, teach us to pray, just as John taught his disciples." He said to them, "When you pray, say: "'Father, hallowed be your name, your kingdom come. Give us each day our daily bread. Forgive us our sins, for we also forgive everyone who sins against us. And lead us not into temptation.'"
>
> Luke 11:1-4

We see examples of Jesus teaching by demonstrating throughout the Scriptures. I offer a time once a week in my office called "Prayer Observatory." In this "class" I simply open up my prayer time and communion with the Lord for observation. I act as if no one else is in the room, and I interact with God as I would any other morning, which is typically pretty verbal. It is *not* so that others would see my prayer life, trust me, it is vulnerable and often feels invasive, but rather I do this so others can learn by seeing. I have had great responses from people throughout the years in regard to the observatory and many have shared specifically how the opportunity to observe has profoundly affected their own communion with God.

i

It is for this purpose that I have included the "Prayer Practices" in this book. They are like mini observatories captured on paper for you. My desire is to demonstrate what it looks like to take a biblical principle and declare it through prayer, thus teaching you how to pray with **authority** and **confidence**. I hope you find them helpful and challenging, and I pray that you will be empowered by them.

Introduction

I originally wrote the message "To Love and To Be Loved" for delivery at a ladies conference in 2016. There was not much specific to establishing healthy relationships in that original message. However, after writing content for a training class titled "Establishing Healthy Relationships," I began to realize that the message of loving and being loved is the key to establishing healthy relationships. Conversely, I also realized that establishing healthy relationships is key in loving and being loved. I therefore concluded that since one without the other is incomplete, this book must contain both topics.

I am often asked what the number one thing is that causes the ladies in our housing program to end up there. The easy and obvious answer is to say, "Poverty barriers." These barriers include mental, emotional, and spiritual instability and a lack of: transportation, childcare, education, housing, and employment. While this answer is accurate, I am realizing more and more that the inability to overcome these barriers is symptomatic. And although we can help them prevail over some of these barriers, there is a much deeper issue at the root: the inability to establish healthy relationships. Not only are most of these ladies unable to establish healthy relationships, most of them can't even define what one looks like. The best they know about relationships is based on the system they were brought up in. This system includes their parents, their friends, their education, their churches, and society as a whole. Isn't this true of us all? We learn to define and assess the health of a relationship based on what we know. Our only frame of reference is what we have lived and experienced. But God has a design in mind for us when it comes to relationships, and it is not like what we find in the world. He has reframed any worldly reference with His supernatural love. This love cannot be comprehended with the natural mind, nor can it be described completely by any human words.

Each one of us is created for relationship. This is why there is a deep desire within all of us for relationship...it is a part of our design. To prosper in life the way God intends; body, soul, and spirit, you must understand His design for relationships and what that means for you. The inability to walk in healthy relationships will dampen the fullness of life and will ultimately leave you dissatisfied.

Relationship is not just about loving others, it is also about being loved by others. We have often heard it asked, "Which is better...to love or to be loved?" It is interesting to me that we try to separate the two. I would even go so far to say that too often the church, or even society, emphasizes the importance of loving more than being loved. I am saddened by the demise of the importance of the God-given value that we are created for both; to love and to be loved. To not allow yourself to be loved according to His design can be just as damaging as not loving others...in fact, I would say it is the number one reason why we ultimately are unable to love others appropriately.

I recently found this quote on the Internet: "To love is nothing. To be loved is something, but to love and to be loved is everything." I think this sums it up well because it embraces the idea of relationship, which ultimately MUST flow two ways. Relationship is meant to be a two-way dynamic. We would all agree that the art of communication involves an exchange of words, a back and forth system where ideas, thoughts, feelings, opinions and such are exchanged. So it should be with relationships. They should include an exchange of love. I like to call it the Love Cycle. In a Love Cycle, we move from loving to being loved, from loving to being loved, over and over within each relationship we have. This is how God created us, with a design to love and to be loved. It is a part of our DNA and how we are wired.

"Let us make man in our own image, according to our likeness..." Genesis 1:26

The Bible tells us several times in 1 John that God is love. He IS love, so to be created in His image means we, too, ARE love. We are loving creatures that carry His love in us. This is a part of who we are in Christ. To live anything less than His design for love is to not live fully.

God not only demonstrates the Love Cycle within the Trinity, but also in that it is His love upon us first that draws the response of our hearts to love Him back. (1 John 4:19) Even science lines up with this Love Cycle by telling us that the best way to experience love or feel love is to express love. So the more we express love, the more we feel love, thus making us not just the giver of love, but the recipient of love as well. So, which is better: to love or to be loved? Yes, please, I'll take both!

So let's circle back to the ladies in our housing program. While there are many skill sets that we can and do teach them, none of them seem to matter if in the end these ladies don't know how to establish and walk in healthy relationships. If they lack the understanding of their design for love and how to enforce that design in their lives, then it is likely that one toxic relationship will restart the poverty cycle.

While not all of us get stuck in circumstantial poverty, many of us are stuck in emotional poverty stemming from unhealthy relationships. We live in fear and often feel victimized or trapped by relationships just like these ladies do by their circumstances. I am burdened for you to know God's design for love and what it looks like within relationships. But I also want to empower you to establish such relationships so that you can walk in the freedom that He intended all along...loving and being loved without any fear, thus enabling you to live life to the fullest.

Section 1 of this book is focused mostly on descriptions and definitions of relationships for the purpose of educating and informing you. As I stated before, I think this knowledge is important to the process of learning how to love and be loved like God designed. Just like with a disease, there are signs and symptoms that we need to recognize to cure the root. In Section 2, I shift into the meat of establishing healthy relationships and the key to loving and being loved freely per God's design.

Section 1

Understanding Relationships:
Getting the Facts and
Becoming Enlightened

Chapter 1
Created for Connection

"Behold I stand at the door and knock. If anyone hears My voice and opens the door, I will come in to him and dine with him, and he with Me" (Revelation 3:20).

God desires to connect with us. The Bible reminds us through this verse that He continually knocks upon the door of our hearts seeking to "come in." Once He connects with us, He can pursue a relationship with us. The imagery of God sitting and eating with us and us with Him was a sign of covenant in the Bible. There are many truths to discern through this single verse, but I want you to see that before we can have a relationship, we must have connection. Relationship requires connection. Or should I say, a HEALTHY relationship requires connection. It is indeed possible to have a relationship without really connecting, but the question is: Is that relationship living in the fullness of God's design? In other words, is it a healthy relationship?

Every human was born with a desire for connection; it is an innate need that we have. Connection is what life is all about; it keeps us going and gives us a sense of belonging. A lack of connection will often lead to emotional detachment, depression, and feelings of rejection, isolation, and deep abandonment. Yet, so many of us fear connection.

TRANSPARENCY AND VULNERABILITY

True connection requires transparency. In order to really connect with someone on a genuine level, you must be able to be the "real you" at all times. There must not be anything kept in the dark, and there must be freedom to be completely honest about all things. I have to be willing to let you see me...all of me...the good, the bad, and the ugly. And that is risky because being

7

transparent makes one vulnerable. I mean think about it, how do I know what you are really going to think if I tell you everything? Will you reject me? Will you judge me? Will you love me? If I want to connect, I must take the risk! I must be vulnerable to the one whom I desire to connect with. Without vulnerability, there will be no genuine connection. Later in this book, we will talk about the importance of self-reconciliation and how that is necessary before true reconciliation with others can take place. Being transparent and vulnerable with others takes much courage. However, your desire to connect must override your fear of "being seen."

THE WOMAN AT THE WELL

Let's take a look at the woman at the well in John Chapter 4. Here we have a woman who had the reputation of being a prostitute. She was so ostracized by society that she came to draw water from the well at high noon, instead of at dawn or dusk like everyone else. The risk of the brutal sun was apparently safer than the risk of being seen or perhaps rejected by others. Let me point out a fact about the culture she lived in. According to the law of the time, only men had the power to marry and divorce. So, although we typically hear about this woman being a prostitute, the truth is she once had five husbands and the man she was currently living with was not her husband. Does this mean she was a prostitute? Or does it mean that she was rejected and abandoned five times? And to add salt to the wound, the man she was currently with was, for whatever reason, unwilling to marry her? Kind of changes your perspective of this woman, doesn't it? We can conclude that this woman likely had a very soft spot in her heart that left her unwilling to expose herself to any more hurts that might come by connecting with others at the well. Running into someone who would know her and her past wasn't worth the risk. Guilt, shame, and rejection kept her from connection because the thought of being exposed was likely too excruciating to her already broken and rejected heart.

But Jesus, in His divine love, pursues connection with her. I love that in John 4:4 we read that Jesus "needed to go through

Samaria." The KJV version reads, "And he must needs go through Samaria." I am not quite sure what that means, but I can take a pretty good guess and say that there was a drawing so hard in His spirit that He HAD to go through Samaria. God, from the very beginning, had a plan for a divine encounter with a woman whom He knew desperately needed to be loved.

So, there is Jesus, sitting by the well when the woman enters into the scene. Upon seeing her, Jesus begins to ask her questions. He asks not just any questions, but *intentional* questions that would expose her need and invite her to connect with Him in that need.   At first she responds by voicing her lack of value. She immediately lets Him know that she is not worthy of connection. Jesus, in His stubborn love, presses in and eventually exposes her deepest need...thirst! He reveals to her that only He can satisfy the REAL need of her thirst. He states: "but whoever drinks of the water that I shall give him will never thirst" (verse 14). He forces her desperation to the surface, still in an effort to connect with her. But note that He then begins to go past her physical thirst and expose her emotional thirst by bringing up her husband. We might say this is cruel, but in reality, it is love. His desire to connect with her motivates Him to invite her to be vulnerable. Her deepest need was also her deepest wound. To expose her need was to expose her wound; and we all know how risky it is to reveal our wounds because they are our weak spots. But Jesus brought up her most vulnerable spot so that ultimately He could connect with her in that place. You see, Jesus knows that connection requires vulnerability.

Just like the woman at the well, we all avoid exposure of our wounds, or weak spots. We will do anything to keep our hurts from being seen. We will talk about our lack of worth, divert questions, or simply avoid the crowd or being around people who might "find us out." But God is a God who pursues His people continually, and He will stop at nothing to connect with you. This is why there is the constant invitation to "come into the light."

"This is the message which we have heard from Him and declare to you, that God is light and in Him is no darkness at all. If we say that

we have fellowship with Him, and walk in darkness, we lie and do not practice the truth. But if we walk in the light as He is in the light, we have fellowship with one another, and the blood of Jesus Christ His Son cleanses us from all sin." 1 John 1:5-7

God Himself walks in the light, making Himself known to us. It is His desire that we would know Him. The knowledge of this truth is what compelled Paul to pray in Ephesians 1:17-19 that the eyes of our hearts would be opened to know Him. He understood that it is God's desire to open His heart and reveal His nature to us. God does not keep His heart from us, instead He wants to show us the fullness of who He is. He knows that to hide His heart would be hindering connection with His children, preventing true fellowship. The Bible says that just as He is, so are we in this world (1 John 4:17), meaning that we too are created to walk in the light of transparency within relationships. Without it, there will be no fellowship with God, with self, or with others!

Since we know that God desires connection, and we know that we are created in His image, then we know that we also desire connection. It is a part of our design in Christ. With that design comes the freedom to be transparent and vulnerable. Later in the book, we will look at the importance of connecting with God, connecting with self, and connecting with others, and how this is imperative in establishing and maintaining healthy relationships. For now, understand that God's definition of a healthy relationship includes connection. Without genuine connection, the relationship falls short of God's design.

PRAYER PRACTICE

God, I thank You that You have created me for connection. I thank You for the gift of fellowship with You first as well as with people. I am forever reminded of the beauty of relationships and forever learning about the perfection of Your design for them.

Thank You for demonstrating that design through Your love

for me and Your pursuit of who I am; that You continue to connect with me in my strengths, in my celebrations, in my weaknesses, and my failures. Thank You for pursuing the hard spots where I need to be loved and for nurturing the soft spots where I need assurance of that love. You amaze me, and in You I find much safety and confidence. May I be a demonstration of what You desire in relationships and may I recognize always the importance of connecting with You, with myself, and with others!

In Jesus' name I pray, Amen.

Part 1
Defining Relationships

Chapter 2
God's Design for Relationships

I think if most of us were honest, we would say that relationships are one of the most challenging things in this life to manage. While some relationships bring much joy, others can bring much heartache. As a certified biblical counselor, you might expect that I spend a lot of time working people through relational issues from their past and their present. What you may not realize is that as a Professional Life Coach, I do much of the same; sometimes in different arenas, such as the workplace or in their profession, but nonetheless, all people struggle with relationships. It is for this purpose that I have spent much of the past few years studying and seeking God on what a healthy relationship really looks like within His design. I believe that even within the church you will find multiple definitions and we certainly know that the world has many as well, but what does God say?

> *"There is no fear in love; but perfect love casts out fear, because fear involves torment. But he who fears has not been made perfect in love." 1 John 4:18*

Can I be honest and tell you that for years I struggled with fear within relationships? The system that I was brought up in taught me that to be loved, you had to do the right things. That love was conditional, and therefore it was based on how well you performed or whether or not your behavior was worthy of love. This fear defined who I was in most of my relationships and navigated the majority of my decisions. I remember clear back in middle school making choices to do things that I did not want to do because of fear of not being liked or accepted.

The word "torment" is a pretty strong word to choose when talking about fear, yet it is one that I think is appropriate. We typically would think about physical torture or agonizing pain when we think about torment. But that is exactly what fear does to us emotionally. Instead of physically torturing us, the enemy emotionally and mentally tortures us. Just like being held hostage and tortured, the enemy wants us to be held hostage and tortured by fear. This is NOT of God! The Bible says that where the spirit of the Lord is, there is liberty (2 Corinthians 3:17).

I experienced this torment when I operated in fear. In fact, torment was at the very root of the clinical depression and panic anxiety attacks that began to manifest in my twenties. The pressure to always do the right thing, to please everyone else, and the striving to be loved and accepted took ahold of me and held me captive. I was unable to make decisions without fear and was always second-guessing myself; criticizing my own actions and performance. Nothing I did was good enough, and my own standards overrode the standards of those around me. I got to an emotional place where I didn't need others to reject me because I lived in self-rejection.

It has been a long process learning how to operate in the freedom of the Lord and getting set free of fear. This process required a lot of reconciliation with God and myself. I had to do this first, and then intentionally change my thought patterns and habits. The key to becoming set free from that fear was recognizing His love and what His love LOOKS like. This will be further explored throughout the book, but what I want you to hear for now is that a healthy relationship is one where there is absolutely no fear.

I am more and more convinced that the greatest sign of excellent health within any relationship is the freedom or the ability to be who you are without fear. A healthy relationship is one where there is never any threat of not being loved or of being rejected in the midst of your transparency. This is God's design. In keeping with this thought as our foundation, let's consider the characteristics of what healthy relationships look like.

EACH PARTY FEELS FREEDOM

Too many times I hear someone say, "But you don't understand, I don't have a choice," or "She/he would be so mad if I didn't___," or "It is just easier to go along with it." Think about your life personally and how many times you make decisions because you feel like you don't have a choice or you feel that you *have* to do something. It can be within a relationship with your spouse or a relationship with your neighbor. It can be a relationship with your co-worker or a relationship with your church. Any time we find ourselves feeling trapped or stuck, we can be sure that it is not God's design.

"The fear of man brings a snare, but whoever trusts in the Lord shall be safe." Proverbs 29:25

EACH PARTY FEELS SAFE AND SECURE

This is more than just physical safety, it includes emotional and mental safety as well. We will talk throughout this book about the power of words and attitudes and their ability to damage the heart and mind. There is more to abuse than use of the fist. When we don't feel safe to simply be real, to share things openly, to express places of vulnerability, there will be a breakdown in connection. This is rooted in the fear of man's response and not in the love of God.

EACH PARTY OWNS UP TO THEIR PART

It is important that each party in a relationship takes responsibility for their own actions. Each should be quick to accept responsibility and receive blame instead of casting the blame on others. People who are unable to admit when they are at fault, or who cannot even clearly see their own faults, are insecure. They will do what is necessary to keep from exposing their own weaknesses. This leads us into the importance for repentance.

REPENTANCE IS NORMAL

Not only should repentance be normal, it should also feel

safe. In a relationship where there is no fear, we can be quick to repent because there is confidence in being forgiven. Any party who is resistant or slow to repent lacks the ability to examine their own heart objectively. Again, this is a sign of fear.

OPEN COMMUNICATION

Relationships should make room for open and honest communication. Each party should feel free to be transparent about what they think, feel, or desire. There should be no fear in expressing oneself freely, completely, and openly. This also means we can freely give and receive feedback without feeling defensive.

EACH PARTY BELIEVES THE BEST

The Bible tells us in 1 Corinthians 13 that *love believes the best*. But too often we assume the worst of others, even within close relationships. This is a judgment of the heart and one that is not of God. Sometimes, in the name of "wisdom" or "discernment" we assume falsely. While it is OK to be wise, love always has hope. Our first response should give the benefit of the doubt and believe God for something good in every person.

EACH PARTY SEEKS TO UNDERSTAND FIRST

When we approach someone in conflict or with an offense, our typical thought is that we want or need them to understand how we feel. A sign of a mature, healthy relationship is that each party seeks to understand the other person *before* they seek to be understood. This is what it means to put the interests of others before your own; you assume the best. I always want to assume that a hurt or offense that I picked up was not intentional, so instead of starting with how I feel, I start with, "Help me understand you." Most often, this instantly softens the hearts of those involved. It can literally change the direction of any conflict towards a healthy conversation.

MUTUAL CARE

Each party should genuinely be interested in meeting the needs of the other. There should be a mutual desire to care for each other. Although the way we care for each other may look different, there should be a mutual care within any relationship. I have several relationships where the other party literally serves me. For example, my assistant and those who work for me were hired to serve me, and they are good at it because they have a gift for helps and/or service. It was hard for me to utilize them at first, and I often felt bugged because I didn't want our relationship to be all about *them* doing for *me*. But after expressing my concern, one of them voiced that they felt that I cared for them just as much, only it looked different. Although it is not my gift to stop by the store for them or help schedule their appointments, it is my gift to pray for them and pastor them through encouragement and counsel. She mentioned that I was the first one everyone went to when they needed advice or prayer, and that in that manner, I was serving and caring for them just as mutually as they cared for me. There should always be a feeling of mutual care within any relationship.

NEITHER PARTY FEELS TAKEN ADVANTAGE OF

This connects with the mutual care. Sometimes, we feel as though we are being taken advantage of, and many times that is true. There should be a sense of partnership within any relationship that leaves both parties feeling important for who they are, not just what they offer. Neither party should feel "taken to the cleaners" or like they are "carrying the weight." Whether it is true or perceived, it is not healthy.

FREE TO SAY NO

It is so important that we feel the freedom to say no in our relationships. This loops back to feeling trapped and stuck; like we *can't* say no, but it also connects with the inability to set healthy boundaries and stick to them. There is fault on both sides when this is the case. Much of what I do is teaching the "weaker" person that their fear of saying no is often their own fault. But either way, it is a sign of an unhealthy relationship.

FREEDOM TO DISAGREE

The world has somehow taught us that a healthy relationship is one where we always agree. This is simply not true. It is, in fact, healthy to feel free to disagree. I tell couples in the counseling room all the time that just because they don't agree on everything does not mean they don't have a healthy marriage. It simply means they are two different people with two different opinions. Good health is seen when both parties feel free to disagree without fear of being loved less or judged. There is a mutual confidence and respect for each party and their opinions, thoughts, and feelings and they are not afraid of conflict. Ultimately, when there is an appreciation for differences, two people end up feeling freer to come to a mutual agreement. This is because there is no threat, or need to be right, involved when we respect each other's differences.

EACH PARTY FEELS CELEBRATED

I think we have, at best, learned how to tolerate others when in reality, God does more than tolerate us...He celebrates us and dotes on our every action. He is enamored by who we are as well as what we do. I think this is one of the ways we can be proactive in pursuing excellent health within our relationships. It is important that our friends, co-workers, children, spouses, and family members feel celebrated. I want all those around me to know that I see them the way God does—with potential and purpose. I want to be known for believing in them and making them feel purposeful and successful. Each life is to be celebrated and a sign of good health is when each party is confident enough in their own successes that they freely can celebrate the other.

NO JEALOUSY

This one is huge. Jealousy is absolutely rooted in fear. Where there is jealousy, there is no freedom. Each party should feel free to spend time with others; furthermore, they should not fear who is invited and who is not. There is also no jealousy of each other's God-accomplishment and dreams, but there is an excitement in seeing each other step into their potential and achievements.

There is no threat of the other person's success in a healthy relationship. Instead, there is mutual honor and respect for the other person's gifts and passions. This goes back to celebrating each other and who you both are!

Although these characteristics do not likely include ALL of what God's design looks like, I would say that it is pretty close. I use this list when assessing the overall health of relationship within my counseling room, and it exposes a lot of brokenness and unhealthy patterns within relationships. Through out this book, you will see hints of these and you will definitely hear me refer to fear a lot, but I felt it important to give a more defined black and white list for those of us who think we don't have unhealthy relationships. Sometimes we need it spelled out for us.

However, in order to come into the fullness of these characteristics, we must start with our own relationship with God and understand His love toward us. What does His love look like? I feel it is best described in 1 Corinthians 13:4-8.

"Love suffers long and is kind; love does not envy; love does not parade itself, is not puffed up; does not behave rudely, does not seek its own, is not provoked, thinks no evil; does not rejoice in iniquity, but rejoices in the truth; bears all things, believes all things, hopes all things, endures all things. Love never fails."

I could list so many other verses that describe what love looks like (and I will throughout the book), however, I believe you will find an element in all the characteristics I listed above right in this one passage. In Section 2, we will discuss in great detail how to establish this way of loving with our goal being to come into His design for healthy relationships.

PRAYER PRACTICE

How beautiful is Your love, O Lord! Who loves like You? Were it not for You, I would know nothing of love and what it looks like. I thank You and praise You for pouring Your love into me and for lavishing me with Your love. I receive Your love that is patient and kind. You do not boast or Lord Yourself over me, You believe the best in me and draw me into Your arms. There is no fear in You, Lord. Your love is freeing and uplifting, and I thank You that You always see and hope for the best in me. I release that kind of love in me, praying that it will flow out of me and onto those around me! Just as I have freely received, may I also freely give. (Matthew 10:8)

In Jesus' name I pray, Amen.

Chapter 3
Forms of Unhealthy Relationships

Over my years of counseling individuals and couples, I have seen many forms of unhealthy relationships. In reality, if the relationship is less than the fullness of God's design, then I would consider it unhealthy. I think as believers we often settle for less than excellent. We serve a God of excellence and He died so that we could live in excellence, but too often we settle in the wilderness and miss out on the milk and the honey. That is His fullness; fullness of life, fullness of health, fullness of potential, and fullness of relationships. Let it be said that just because you may not fall into the category of these unhealthy relationships that we are about to discuss does not mean that you are experiencing the most excellent design within all of your relationships. That should be our goal; I know it is mine. I have some great relationships, but my desire is always to intentionally strive towards excellence in them all. Part of this means I need to be able to recognize unhealthy patterns and characteristics of unhealthy relationships. My goal is that you fall in love with the beauty of God's design and equip you to pursue that design.

SOUL TIES

"And it came to pass, when he had made an end of speaking unto Saul, that the soul of Jonathan was knit with the soul of David, and Jonathan loved him as his own soul." 1 Samuel 18:1

I love the storyline of David and Jonathan. Here we have a young man (Jonathan) whose lineage made him the rightful heir to the kingship. However, Jonathan understood that it was God's will for David to be the next king. The beauty of this relationship is that Jonathan, instead of responding in envy or anger, willingly surrendered his position. He actually gave David his clothes and military tools, we read in 1 Samuel 18:4. Can I be honest and say that if I were Jonathan, I think I would have been a little bit salty about the fact that David was positioned for what was rightfully supposed to be mine? This is a great example of a person demonstrating the ability to celebrate another's purpose instead of feeling threatened by it. We see the two of them express their loyalty to each other and to God's will for David's kingship throughout the story, and it ends with an act that demonstrates the freedom they had in expressing their emotions. Nowhere in the relationship was there any dominance, control, manipulation, or fear. Instead, "In honor, giving preference to one another" (Romans 12:10) there was an awareness of each other's "God design" and who they were called to be. They had confidence in God's plan and preferred that plan over their own interests. This is why they'd be willing to lay their lives down for each other. This is a great example of a Godly soul-tie.

Any time two souls tightly knit together; there is a soul-tie. This can be the case in any friendship and certainly should be the case in a marriage. Just like with David and Jonathan, there is freedom in the connection and mutual understanding of each other's God-purpose and life's goals. And just like we discussed in Chapter 2, there is a mutual desire to protect and nurture that person into their purpose.

God has designed soul-ties so that we can connect with others in our soul-realm. I use this term to define a relationship that is truly within God's design. There can be much joy in a Godly soul-tie because it is God-ordained and God-centered. However, the connection must remain God-focused, otherwise our own flesh will get tangled up in there, which can often shift into an ungodly soul-tie.

UNGODLY SOUL-TIES

It is fair to say that any relationship not operating within God's design is an ungodly soul-tie. It is the broadest definition of an unhealthy relationship. An ungodly soul-tie is exactly the opposite of what we just discussed. It is when two people are knit in the soul to the point that they put that person before God. It can be two-way, or just one-way. Either way, at the core, the relationship is navigated by fear. I see this in female friendships a lot. When you act and respond out of the needs, actions, or emotions of the other, then that person becomes your god. You let that person navigate your choices, emotions, thoughts, etc. Ungodly soul-ties are a form of idolatry when you live your life in response to that person instead of to God.

An example of this is found in Genesis 29 with Leah and her desire to please Jacob. She took the blessings of God (her babies) and used them to try and win over the love of Jacob. This manipulation was motivated by her fear. She desperately wanted to be loved by him and was seeking his approval. In the end, we see her shift to responding to God's love instead of Jacob's.

"When the Lord saw that Leah was unloved, He opened her womb; but Rachel was barren. So Leah conceived and bore a son, and she called his name Reuben; for she said, "The Lord has surely looked on my affliction. Now therefore, my husband will love me." Then she conceived again and bore a son, and said, "Because the Lord has heard that I am unloved, He has therefore given me this son also." And she called his name Simeon. She conceived again and bore a son, and said, "Now this time my husband will become attached to me, because I have borne him three sons." Therefore his name was called Levi. And she conceived again and bore a son, and said, "Now I will praise the Lord." Therefore she called his name Judah. Then she stopped bearing."

How far do we go to help or please others? This is a difficult thing to discern, and I think it is too often taught that we should simply lay our lives down for the needs of others without wisdom or healthy boundaries.

"For do I now persuade men, or God? Or do I seek to please men? For if I still pleased men, I would not be a bondservant of Christ." Galatians 1:10

Leah was living her life for Jacob, and her motive was not to please God, but to please man. This is not the action of a bondservant, but rather just a servant. A servant is one who is forced to serve another, whereas, a bondservant is a servant who has been set free, but chooses of his own free will to stay and serve. You see, the motive of the service is completely different!

When we live our lives to please others first instead of God first, we will find ourselves in an idolatrous situation. While God does indeed ask us to "esteem others better than ourselves" (Phil. 2:3), He does not want us to put their interests before His or forget our own, for that matter (Phil 2:4). It is not about putting their interest first, nor is it about putting our interest first, but rather, it is about putting God's interest first. That's what Jonathan and David did. I will expand this religious conundrum later in the book when we look at the importance of self-love and self-care and how it is crucial in loving others more effectively.

CODEPENDENCY

Codependency is a more defined form of an ungodly soul-tie. It is typically one-way in that one party is codependent on the other, but it can work in both directions. At the core of co-dependency is enablement.

According to Wikipedia, codependency is a type of dysfunctional helping relationship where one person supports or enables another person's drug addiction, alcoholism, gambling addiction, poor mental health, immaturity, irresponsibility, or under-achievement. However, the term has been broadened to describe several types of destructive relationship patterns. I have heard codependency referred to as "relationship addiction" which greatly broadens the definition. It is a learned behavior (as are all unhealthy relationships) that is typically passed down through generations and establishes a pattern of placing God second to people.

Codependents often take on a martyr's role and become "benefactors" to the "afflicted" party. This means they continue to make excuses for them and actually thrive off of the needs that party has for their constant help. They are loyal in a destructive way that only further enables the "afflicted" party. This emotional and behavioral condition affects each party's ability to have a healthy, mutually-satisfying relationship. It is not God's design!

ABUSIVE RELATIONSHIPS

This is a hot topic for me. I think that society has boxed the concept of abuse to mean that one has been physically beaten or hurt. There are many forms of abuse other than just physical, such as emotional, mental, and verbal abuse. The old adage, "Sticks and stones may break my bones, but names will never hurt me," is not only *not* true, it is not biblical! Yet, we teach that to our children in hopes that they will learn to brush off the words of others. And I get it. The intent is good, but the outcome has not been so good. It has inadvertently taught us that there is no power in words, which is simply not true.

It is one thing to teach children how to deal with negative words; it is another to teach them to simply ignore the emotions that negative words come with. One leads to teaching what is and what is not OK, while empowering children to set healthy boundaries, whereas the other teaches avoidance and ignorance. Instead of raising up a culture that can handle conflict and deal honestly with those who use words to wound, we do one of two things, we either handle the words with aggression, and respond with defense and anger, or we settle into silence, thus positioning ourselves to be more victimized. There will be an entire section of this book devoted to setting healthy boundaries, but for now let me say that the inability to set healthy boundaries leads to feelings of victimization, and your defeat will leave you angry and bitter.

If I had to summarize abuse, I would say that it is any relationship where there is power, control, and misuse of authority at play. This can be within a marriage, any friendship, with a family member, or a co-worker. It is important to note that just as often as we dismiss emotionally-abusive relationships, we often call things emotional abuse when they are not.

A relationship that includes heated discussions where there is yelling and screaming does not make it emotionally abusive, it just means those involved don't know the art of healthy communication. It is important to remember that at the root of abuse is control and power!

Although we typically hear about one party being the abuser and one being the victim, with emotional and verbal abuse it can go both ways. I have seen many relationships, from marital to a mother and her daughter, where both parties seek to control each other through criticism, belittling comments, and manipulative behaviors. Often this becomes the "personality" of the relationship and both parties think it is normal, although they operate constantly both in fear and deception. There is no transparency because remember, transparency means vulnerability, and where there is vulnerability, there is an open door for one person to take advantage. Many relationships operate in mutual emotional abuse.

GASLIGHTING

I really want to spend some time informing you about gaslighting because I feel it is the most common form of abuse that we come up against in the counseling room today. The term "gaslighting" can be traced back to a 1938 play. British playwright Patrick Hamilton created "Gas Light," a mystery/thriller that premiered in London and played there for six months. In 1944, there was a film adaptation of the play called "Gaslight." The play is about a married couple named Paula and Gregory. Throughout the film, abusive husband Gregory manipulates Paula to make her feel as if she has gone mad. He leads her to believe she's stealing things without realizing it and hearing noises that aren't really there. Paula begins to question her reality. Although this play depicts an extreme case, there are subtle forms of gaslighting that I encounter almost weekly within the counseling room.

Simply said, gaslighting is a form of emotional abuse where one party manipulates things to trick or twist someone into distrusting or doubting his or her own memory, perceptions, and sanity. It is an insidious form of abuse that is very subtle, and therefore easily misread. It can start out very gradually, but over time has harmful effects. While some gaslighters are intentional, for many it is simply their only knowledge of how a relationship is supposed to work. We see this in children who were raised by parents who manipulated them into obedience, or taught them that to be loved, they had to be or act a certain way. Their parents used fear to control them. Those children often grow up to learn to get what they want by twisting or manipulating things in their direction. This is their only frame of reference for relationships. When they use that technique to gain control over another person, it is gaslighting.

So, let's take a moment to be honest, we all have our own "gaslighting" tendencies and tactics. Whether we realize it or not, the flesh likes to manipulate to get what we want!

"What causes fights and quarrels among you? Don't they come from your desires that battle within you? You desire but do not have, so you kill. You covet but you cannot get what you want, so you quarrel and fight. You do not have because you do not ask God. When you ask, you do not receive, because you ask with wrong motives, that you may spend what you get on your pleasures." James 4:1-3 (NIV)

We have all heard the term "narcissism." A narcissist is a person who has an excessive interest in or admiration of himself or herself. Biblically, it is self-idolatry. Kind of simplifies it, eh? At the root of gaslighting is self-idolatry, or an inflated view of self. God addresses this time and time again in the Bible. Why? Because He knows that the tendency of our flesh is selfish, haughty, and egotistical.

"Do nothing out of selfish ambition or vain conceit. Rather, in humility value others above yourselves, not looking to your own interests but each of you to the interests of the others. In your relationships with one another, have the same mindset as Christ Jesus." Philippians 2:3-5

"For I say, through the grace given to me, to everyone who is among you, not to think of himself more highly than he ought to think, but to think soberly, as God has dealt to each one a measure of faith." Romans 12:3

Again, while I do not want to diminish the severity of gaslighting and the damage it can do, I also want you to realize how innate it is for all of us to operate in ways that are selfish. I say this to challenge you to consider ways that you may tend toward unintentionally gaslighting people in order to get your way or to take or keep control.

Let's circle back to the more damaging cases of gaslighting. Here are the "victim signs" that I use to assess gaslighting within a relationship. I am simply going to list these out for you to ponder.

1. You constantly second-guess yourself.
2. You question if you are too sensitive.
3. You often feel confused and have a hard time making simple decisions.
4. You tend to feel like you're under a "fog" or that your thoughts are foggy or less clear than typical.
5. You find yourself constantly apologizing.
6. You can't understand why you're so unhappy or you feel depressed.
7. You often make excuses for your partner's behavior.
8. You feel like you can't do anything right.
9. You often feel like you aren't good enough for others.
10. You have a sense that you used to be a more confident, relaxed, and happy person.
11. You withhold information from friends and family so you don't have to explain things.

I want to be sure you understand that many victims of gaslighting position themselves in the victim position. I do not say that to victim-blame, but rather to empower the victim. Typically the victim has not been taught to set healthy boundaries, and therefore they are easy targets or easily manipulated. They also tend to be the "nice guy" that every one ends up pushing around. Remember what I talked about at the very beginning of this abusive section? We are not taught how to deal with those who verbally assault us, but instead we are taught to be passive and "put up with it" or ignore it. I am not suggesting that we teach kids to respond with anger or aggression, but I am saying that we should teach them how to set healthy boundaries.

MIDDLE SCHOOL BULLY

My daughter is in middle school, and like many middle schoolers, she is part of a group of girls that hang out together. In this little group, there is one girl in particular who is dominant and tends to be mean to all the others. She is rude and often criticizes or cuts the other girls down, and when they are in a group, she seeks control. When she doesn't get her way, she gets mad and won't talk to whoever has told her, "no" and she tries to recruit the other girls to side with her. She is an emotional bully, and the other girls would find themselves frustrated and tiptoeing around her.

Following a recent conflict with this young lady, my daughter expressed that she felt freedom in the fact that this girl was not currently talking to her. I have watched this young lady in our home and have seen how she dominates and manipulates. Of course my flesh wanted to tell my daughter to not be her friend and be done with her, or I wanted to pick up an offense and begin to criticize this young lady to my daughter. However, I saw a teaching opportunity. My daughter is empathetic, which means she can be easily emotionally manipulated. I recognized that it was time to teach her how to deal lovingly with those who mistreat her or try to emotionally control her. I encouraged her to understand her friend's heart and consider her family structure (which is not stable). We concluded that her friend operated in fear of not being loved or accepted and that drove some of her behaviors. We also concluded that she did not have many examples of what a healthy relationship should look like. I asked my daughter to think about whether or not her friendship was worth honesty. My daughter said yes. (YAAAAY!) We then discussed why her friend's behavior was not in God's design for friendship. I worked to shift my daughter's heart from being personally offended by her friend to being burdened for her heart. This was not about defending my daughter, but rather defending God's design!

I am proud to say that my daughter went and spoke honestly to her friend about her behavior and how it is not who she is in Christ. She was able to give specific examples of how her friend offended God's design and told her that she would not allow it anymore. She told her that if she is rude to her or makes her feel "cut down" that she would immediately tell her that her words and attitude are not OK and that she would be leaving until the friend could be more respectful. Her friend cried and said that she didn't realize what she was doing and that she didn't mean it. My daughter was able to connect with her friend's heart that day on a new level. There was risk involved in being that transparent and vulnerable, but she decided that it was worth the risk. She wanted a relationship, but she wanted it to be healthy.

THE SPIRIT OF GASLIGHTING

I believe that behind every behavior, there is a spirit at work. Sometimes the spirit is of God, and sometimes it is of Satan. This being said, we see evidence of a gaslighting spirit throughout the Bible. Because it is such a hard spirit to discern, I want to give you two examples from Scripture so you can see how sly and savvy this spirit works. I am also doing this so you can see that it IS indeed a spirit and it needs to be dealt with as such. As I stated before, many "gaslighters" are not even aware of their behavior and the stronghold that it is in their lives. Most often the spirit of gaslighting is self-idolatry, which can be rooted in fear or pride. Therefore, our goal should not be to come against the person, but rather to help them come out from the stronghold of that spirit. Our enemy is never flesh and blood, so we should never consider "people" the battle.

"For we do not wrestle against flesh and blood, but against principalities, against powers, against the rulers of the darkness of this age, against spiritual hosts of wickedness in the heavenly places." Ephesians 6:12

The first example is the classic story of the Fall and the deception of Eve in the Garden of Eden. After learning more about what gaslighting looks like, read through this passage with your eyes opened to the spirit.

"Now the serpent was more cunning than any beast of the field which the Lord God had made. And he said to the woman, "Has God indeed said, 'You shall not eat of every tree of the garden'?" And the woman said to the serpent, "We may eat the fruit of the trees of the garden; but of the fruit of the tree which is in the midst of the garden, God has said, 'You shall not eat it, nor shall you touch it, lest you die.' "Then the serpent said to the woman, "You will not surely die. For God knows that in the day you eat of it your eyes will be opened, and you will be like God, knowing good and evil."
Genesis 3:1-5

I think it is interesting to note that the word *cunning* here is often interpreted as the word *subtle*, which is a classic trait of gaslighting. Recall this definition of gaslighting:

"Gaslighting is a form of emotional abuse where one party manipulates things to trick or twist someone into distrusting or doubting his or her own memory, perceptions, and sanity. It is an insidious form of abuse that is very subtle, and therefore easily misread. It can start out very gradually, but over time has harmful effects."

Do you see it? Satan is the author of the gaslighting spirit and he is a master at gaslighting people. He will twist the truth to get you to doubt your own confidence and allure you into compromising your thoughts, opinions, and feelings. Ultimately he wants to change your mind about what you once believed to be true and in the end steal your identity.

Another example where we see clearly the characteristics of a gaslighting spirit is in Isaiah 36 through a man (the Rabshakeh) who came into Judah on behalf of Sennacherib, the king of Assyria. The people of Judah were under the leadership of Hezekiah, who had led them according to the Lord. But listen to some of the things that were spoken to the people of Judah and the subtle ways he tries to get the people to question, or doubt, their confidence in their king, their ally, but mostly in their God. He mocks them and taunts them and then presents himself as their "hero."

Then the Rabshakeh said to them, "Say now to Hezekiah, 'Thus says the great king, the king of Assyria: "What confidence is this in which you trust? I say you speak of having plans and power for war; but they are mere words. Now in whom do you trust, that you rebel against me? Look! You are trusting in the staff of this broken reed, Egypt, on which if a man leans, it will go into his hand and pierce it. So is Pharaoh king of Egypt to all who trust in him. "But if you say to me, 'We trust in the Lord our God,' is it not He whose high places and whose altars Hezekiah has taken away, and said to Judah and Jerusalem, 'You shall worship before this altar'?"'

Now therefore, I urge you, give a pledge to my master the king of Assyria, and I will give you two thousand horses—if you are able on your part to put riders on them! How then will you repel one captain of the least of my master's servants, and put your trust in Egypt for chariots and horsemen? Have I now come up without the Lord against this land to destroy it? The Lord said to me, 'Go up against this land, and destroy it.'" Then Eliakim, Shebna, and Joah said to the Rabshakeh, "Please speak to your servants in Aramaic, for we understand it; and do not speak to us in Hebrew in the hearing of the people who are on the wall." But the Rabshakeh said, "Has my master sent me to your master and to you to speak these words, and not to the men who sit on the wall, who will eat and drink their own waste with you?"

Then the Rabshakeh stood and called out with a loud voice in Hebrew, and said, "Hear the words of the great king, the king of Assyria! Thus says the king: 'Do not let Hezekiah deceive you, for he will not be able to deliver you; nor let Hezekiah make you trust in the Lord, saying, "The Lord will surely deliver us; this city will not be given into the hand of the king of Assyria."' Do not listen to Hezekiah; for thus says the king of Assyria: 'Make peace with me by a present and come out to me; and every one of you eat from his own vine and every one from his own fig tree, and every one of you drink the waters of his own cistern; until I come and take you away to a land like your own land, a land of grain and new wine, a land of bread and vineyards. Beware lest Hezekiah persuade you, saying,

"The Lord will deliver us." Has any one of the gods of the nations delivered its land from the hand of the king of Assyria? Where are the gods of Hamath and Arpad? Where are the gods of Sepharvaim? Indeed, have they delivered Samaria from my hand? Who among all the gods of these lands have delivered their countries from my hand, that the Lord should deliver Jerusalem from my hand."'
Isaiah 36:4-20

After mocking them, taunting them, and twisting truths, he then presents himself as their ally and like he is their only option. In fact, he speaks as though he wants to rescue them and protect them. It caused them to feel as though they NEEDED him, and that without him, they would be defeated. This is classic of a gaslighting spirit. This spirit loves to be the hero and make its "prey" feel totally dependent on him. They often allure you in by presenting to be your friend and the one who cares and knows best.

Here is how Sennacherib is presented in the account from 2 Chronicles 32:1.

"After these deeds of faithfulness, Sennacherib king of Assyria came and entered Judah; he encamped against the fortified cities, thinking to win them over to himself."

Look at the motive: "to win them over to himself." Remember Philippians 2: "Do nothing out of selfish ambition or vain conceit"? Need I say more? Note: The Pharisees and Sadducees had spirits of gaslighting.

Although these two stories are extreme cases of gaslighting, I believe it is important to acknowledge that this spirit is an age-old spirit; there is nothing new under the sun (Ecclesiastes 1:9). Paul warns the Corinthians of this spirit.

"But I fear, lest somehow, as the serpent deceived Eve by his craftiness, so your minds may be corrupted from the simplicity of Christ." 2 Corinthians 11:3

We can be sure that God is familiar with this spirit. This means that the blood of His Son, Jesus, covers this spirit just like any others that we face today in our culture. We must learn to recognize these spirits and stand in the authority that we have to say no to their control and attempts to steal our identities.

SPIRITUAL ABUSE

In keeping in line with the fact that abuse basically comes down to control, power, and a misuse of authority, spiritual abuse occurs when any religious belief is used to gain control over someone. This includes using the Bible to gain control. Like all abuse, this could mean mentally, emotionally, physically or even sexually. We have seen cases where a man uses the biblical interpretation he has been taught by the church to "have his own way" with his wife sexually. And because it is what they have been taught, they both believe it is OK, even though the wife feels controlled and fears saying no to her husband. This is NOT OK! This is a very real problem.

There is a common doctrine in many churches that teaches that the man is the head of the marriage, and while I agree with this concept, what it looks like often gets skewed and taken to an unhealthy level. Too often, it is taught that it means the husband is to "stay in control" of his wife and that he has the final say in everything. The problem becomes that often the wife is not considered nor is she even given an opinion. There can be a real loss of identity for her in that she is not given a voice and when she speaks, she is disregarded or silenced. In such cases, she can become somewhat robotic in her role, which starts to look subordinate or "less than." There is dismissal in the importance of her role in the body. The body contains the heart, and the last I looked, the head and the heart, though they function differently, are both vital to the health of the body as a whole.

There is a difference between swooning someone to submit and forcing them to submit. God never forces His authority on us, nor does He force us to submit to Him; if He did, we wouldn't have free will. He has given us free will because He wants us to CHOOSE Him. There is no fear or lording of authority, but rather a drawing

to surrender through His unconditional love.
"The Lord has appeared of old to me, saying: 'Yes, I have loved you with an everlasting love; Therefore with lovingkindness I have drawn you.'" Jeremiah 31:3

I wrote about this same concept briefly in my book *Mastering Your Seasons.*

I recently heard a sermon where the pastor described the verbiage on a sign that had been placed by a bed of flowers. The sign was written in three different languages. The first was in German and read, "Picking flowers is prohibited." The second was in English and read, "Please don't pick the flowers." The third was in French and it read, "If you love the flowers, you won't pick them."

Through the three different languages, the message was the same. The difference is that the first conveyed the idea of obedience out of fear of authority. Prohibition promotes fear and intimidation. The second pulls on one's desire to be pleasing and "do the right thing." It feeds on your fear of what others would think and the desire to please people. But the third reminds the passer-by that if you love the flowers, then you won't pick them. It draws out the motive of love by reminding you that to pick the flowers would ultimately kill them.

And so it should be with the Lover of your Soul. Everything you do should be motivated by love, first and foremost. This requires falling in love with Him first. He sets you up to fall deeply into that place at times by alluring you into intimacy.

While fear can and does motivate people, it is not a healthy form of motivation. It tends to simply intimidate, and God is not an intimidator, He is a Lover, and remember, His perfect love casts out fear (1 John 4:18). It is by His love that we are allured into submission and swoon to follow. This is the example that we have of a healthy marriage, one where the motive of everything we do is love.

No person, counselor, system, or doctrine should define anyone's relationship, including that within a marriage. I believe the husband and wife get to decide what their roles look like and those roles should be established based on who they are, their individual strengths and weaknesses, and what they each want. Both parties should feel freedom, without any hint of power, control, or fear. If one marriage decides he has the final say in everything and they both agree to that and she still feels treasured and cared for, great! If another marriage decides they want to partner in every decision and they are able to do so in a way that they both feel treasured and cared for, great! In some marriages, he has final say of the finances, in some she does... as long as in both cases this is what THEY have decided and they both feel loved in those roles. We must not lose our freedom of choice when establishing the personality of any relationship, especially within marriage. Being navigated by systems, traditions, and doctrines is not practicing the power of choice and it will lead to a stripping of freedom within your relationships.

Too often we experience fear within religious teachings. Often the Bible or religious beliefs are used as a reason to "rightfully" condemn or judge someone and instead of feeling loved and lifted up (even in discipline), we feel cut down and scolded. We are not taught to obey out of love, but rather out of fear, which gives a false understanding of love, which is the essence of God's nature. This obviously has a profound effect on our relationships. If we don't understand His love within us first, how in the world will we get it right in our relationships around us?

In Section 2, you will learn that the first step to loving others and being loved by others (establishing healthy relationships) is to be reconciled with who God is and His love. It is through the solid foundation of being reconciled with His love first that you will truly operate in love with others without fear and you can overcome any form of poor health within all your relationships. Hang with me... we are getting to the meat of the matter!

PRAYER PRACTICE

God, thank You that there is no fear with You! Thank You that You have led me into a greater understanding of Your love and that Your love draws me daily to follow Your heart in all things. Thank You that I find safety and confidence in Your Presence and that Your love covers up a multitude of sins, flaws, and failures (1 Peter 4:8). Your love sees the best and believes the best in me (1 Corinthians 13:7) and by Your love I am becoming my best! Thank You Father for seeking me out daily and for never giving up on me!

In Jesus' name I pray, Amen.

Part 2
Redefining Relationships

Chapter 4
Ready for Change

Is it possible to change relationships that have been stuck in unhealthy patterns, even if they've been that way for many years? Do we have any power or choices in the matter? Can one person in the relationship change the pattern or the personality of the relationship? The answer is yes! But, as I mentioned previously, when you decide to start redefining a relationship, there is risk involved.

I mentioned in the previous chapter that abuse is a hot topic for me. This is because I see forms of emotional abuse and gaslighting at the root of almost every unhealthy relationship. And to top it off, the lines of this kind of abuse can be so fuzzy that it is often not easily recognized; and when it is, no one knows how to deal with it effectively. We either dismiss it, or we run from it. This is not only the case in ordinary relationships; it is also the case within marriages.

Let it be said that I highly honor the emotional well-being of people; it is what I do for a living. I help people come into the fullness of life, body, soul and spirit. This means living emotionally healthy lives. I say this because I fear that the church too often prioritizes the sanctity of marriage over the sanity of life. I am not saying that we should jump into a divorce in cases of emotional abuse, but I am saying that those being abused don't have to put up with it. There is a middle ground, and it is called setting healthy boundaries and consequences. I have seen many marriages shattered because instead of teaching one to set boundaries and "hold the line" on how people are meant to be treated, they are counseled to simply be quiet and pray that their gaslighting/emotionally abusive spouse will change. This often leads to the victim feeling defeated or justified to simply run and escape the marriage.

So where do we begin? Well, I have a lot to say on this matter, so let me back up and break it down. Remember, what you are about to read is not limited to marriages, but it does include marriages; meaning you absolutely can implement and practice redefining habits in all of your relationships!

Now, remember, this whole first section is simply about equipping you with practical knowledge and tools to establish healthy relationships, but the key is found in Section 2 where we will learn how to love and be loved through true spiritual reconciliation. It is through reconciliation that God changes us on the inside and transforms who we are and how we think. But we must also train towards righteousness by learning and implementing new patterns in our words, actions, thoughts, feelings, and behaviors. In other words, we partner with God to enforce the life changes needed to establish healthy relationships. This is why one section without the other would be incomplete. With that all said, let's proceed!

YOUR RELATIONSHIP PATTERN

I have mentioned before we are brought up under a system that is a combination of all the influences that we are exposed to such as our family, our teachers, our church, our peers, our community, where we live, etc. It is this system and our place within it that helps to mold us into who we are and the patterns that we develop throughout life. In other words, the way that I am raised has an effect on who I am and the way I think, feel, and respond to life. While I bring my own set of patterns into every relationship, the other party in the relationship brings their own set, and together we create new patterns within our relationship. Over time, the relationship develops a "personality" of its own. I know that is personifying the relationship, but in a sense each relationship we have has its own look, or personality if you will. The point is that we as individuals each help to create the personality of every relationship, and that personality, just like our personality, is made up of patterns and behaviors. If you don't like the way the personality of a relationship has shaped up, you have the power to change it by changing patterns.

DEFINING THE PERSONALITY

While there are many ways to define the current personality of a particular relationship, I once heard it broken down into these three categories: difficult, disappointing, or destructive. Ask yourself which category you are in when you are feeling less than satisfied in any one relationship. Many people don't want to face the fact that a relationship may be destructive. On the other hand, you may have assumed that a relationship is destructive when in reality it is simply just disappointing or difficult. By honestly defining your relationship, you will be able to better understand the heart of the problem.

Understanding the heart of the problem will help you attack it more effectively because you will know in advance what character you personally need to work on through the redefining process.

"My brethren, count it all joy when you fall into various trials, knowing that the testing of your faith produces patience. But let patience have its perfect work, that you may be perfect and complete, lacking nothing." James 1:2-4

God allows challenges, especially through relationships, to refine us and bring us into His perfection. He is a God who loves us so much that He is unwilling to leave us incomplete. Instead, He uses circumstances and people to mold us and give us opportunity to learn and practice His character. Knowing this, if a relationship is difficult, you can seek God for perseverance and patience. You can expect that those qualities will likely be challenged because God desires to perfect them in you. Similarly, if the relationship is disappointing, you can be sure that God will be working out rejection, faintheartedness, and weariness in you. If you feel the relationship is destructive, you should reflect back on the forms of unhealthy relationships. Is the relationship destructive physically, emotionally, mentally, or spiritually? If you are currently in a physically destructive relationship, please take time right now to seek outside help and safety before you proceed in making any changes to your relationship. If you feel your relationship is destructive, but not physically, then you can be sure that God will be rising you up into a new boldness and will be shaving off fear and intimidation through the redefining process.

REDEFINING THE PATTERN

"And do not be conformed to this world, but be transformed by the renewing of your mind, that you may prove what is that good and acceptable and perfect will of God." Romans 12:2

In Romans 12:2 we are reminded that we are to no longer be conformed to this world. This includes the patterns or blueprints that have been impressed upon us through that system. But remember, we have helped to create our own patterns. Sometimes I call these gridlines in our brains. Over time, the same thought patterns, or behaviors, have created ruts in our minds that we then get stuck in. This is what we would call strongholds because they have a strong hold on our minds and alter God's design for us.

You need to create new ruts by intentionally changing your thoughts and behaviors. This is what it means to be transformed by the renewing of the mind. I mentioned earlier that God supernaturally transforms you on the inside through His power. He literally drops the mind of Christ into you when you accept Jesus as your Savior. The Holy Spirit takes up residence in your life. However, you must train yourself to line up with His mind through a renewing process. The word "renewal" in the Greek language means "renovation, or a complete change for the better." When a person renovates a house, there is an outcome in mind. There is a final product that the builder is working toward. In order for that outcome to play out, there is work to do, and that work involves removing some things and rebuilding other things. This is exactly what it means to renew the mind; there are some thought patterns and behaviors that need to be completely removed, and new patterns that need to be built. Just like

46

renovating a house takes daily consistency of intentional work, so does renewing the mind.

When we work toward changing our patterns within relationships, the outcome proves God's most excellent design for love, which is that "good and acceptable and perfect will of God" that we are after. Remember, at the core of who we are, we all want to love and to be loved!

It is great when I counsel two people and they both agree that they don't like the current personality of their relationship and they both want to partner on working toward a more excellent design! In most marriage counseling sessions, this is the case. When I can get the couple to agree, then they are on the same side working toward a common goal, which is God's design for them; the "good and acceptable and perfect will of God."

GADGETS AND GEARS

One of the pictures that God has given me as a visual for a relationship is that of a machine. A machine is an apparatus using or applying mechanical power and having several parts, each with a definite function. Together they perform a particular task. I want you to think with me about those little toys that included gears and gadgets that you put on a "platform" of some sort to create a machine. The edge of each gear fits snuggly into another one. This causes them to move together, even when only one is physically moved. When several of these gadgets and gears are put together, they create a cause and effect relationship. To spin one causes movement in all the others and affects the whole machine. This is what a relationship looks like, and very much how it works. Every action that I make, every word that I use, every behavior I display is like a gear within the relationship that causes an effect on the other gears. Like a machine, a relationship is made up of many gadgets and gears that each party brings to the relationship. With every action that each party makes, there is a reaction from the other party. This can be a good thing in that you have the power to enforce change in your relationships by changing the way you "spin." However, you must also be aware of how you are tempted to be "moved" by the behaviors of others.

MIRRORING SPIRITS

It is good to be aware that you tend to act or behave within relationships based on how the other party acts. Think about those gears, if one spins right, the other spins left. We call this mirroring spirits. You mirror another when you respond to anger with anger, to defense with defense, to silence with silence, to rejection with rejection. I react, you react, you react, I react... I spin left, you spin right, you spin left, I spin right. To every action within a relationship, there is a reaction, and the tendency of our flesh is to respond to flesh with flesh. Jesus actually attacks this fleshly instinct by challenging us to love our enemies.

"But I say to you who hear: Love your enemies, do good to those who hate you, bless those who curse you, and pray for those who spitefully use you. To him who strikes you on the one cheek, offer the other also. And from him who takes away your cloak, do not withhold your tunic either. Give to everyone who asks of you. And from him who takes away your goods do not ask them back. And just as you want men to do to you, you also do to them likewise.
"But if you love those who love you, what credit is that to you? For even sinners love those who love them. And if you do good to those who do good to you, what credit is that to you? For even sinners do the same. And if you lend to those from whom you hope to receive back, what credit is that to you? For even sinners lend to sinners to receive as much back. But love your enemies, do good, and lend, hoping for nothing in return; and your reward will be great, and you will be sons of the Most High. For He is kind to the unthankful and evil. Therefore be merciful, just as your Father also is merciful."
Luke 6:27-36

Let's be honest, this is hard! This whole passage challenges me personally because it requires laying my life down. It means I cannot respond according to how I feel, but rather according to God's heart.

PRAYER PRACTICE

I must stop, Father, and respond to You in prayer. This passage is so challenging and yet so inspiring at the same time. Thank You that You have called me to live a higher calling and not to live according to the ways of the world. I loosen Your love in me, that I would be compelled to love like this. May I do good to ALL, especially those who are against me or who hurt me. I give You my heart, that in all things and in all relationships, my motive would always be love. Use me, Lord, as Your vessel. My life is not my own, but it is Yours to do what You will. May I always adhere to Your example of love.

In Jesus' name I pray, Amen.

I could fill the next ten pages of this book with Scriptures that encourage us to love and respond the way God does. When I read those verses, I am always challenged because it is hard not to mirror the spirit that I am encountering in the person I am dealing with. But if we are going to change the pattern of our relationships, we have to start by changing the way *we* respond to those we deal with.

MIRRORING JESUS

Instead of mirroring the spirit of people, we must learn to mirror Jesus. There is one spirit that matters and trumps every other spirit and that is the Holy Spirit. The Holy Spirit was manifest to His fullest through the life of Jesus Christ. His nature, His character, and His heart was seen in the way Jesus lived. We would do well to learn from the way Jesus interacts with others in the gospels; how He talks, how He loves, His patience, and His kindness. He does not treat others according to their flesh, or His flesh for that matter, but rather according to His heart. This is our example! And though it is a challenge, we have been empowered through the presence of the Holy Spirit, who lives within us as believers, to live like Christ. We must keep in mind that we are no longer living for ourselves, but for Him who died for us! And the more you comprehend His love for you, the more it will become your desire to surrender to His nature.

"For the love of Christ compels us, because we judge thus: that if One died for all, then all died; and He died for all, that those who live should live no longer for themselves, but for Him who died for them and rose again. Therefore, from now on, we regard no one according to the flesh. Even though we have known Christ according to the flesh, yet now we know Him thus no longer."
2 Corinthians 5:14-16

Notice that this passage says that it is *His* love that compels us, not religion or guilt or condemnation... or even my own flesh and my selfish desire to want to "look" like a Christian. But rather Scripture tells us that the more we comprehend His love for us, the more it will become our desire to surrender to His nature within us. The result is the "therefore." *"Therefore, from now on we regard no one according to the flesh."* We are able to look past their fleshy behaviors of anger, defense, self-pity, pride, rejection, etc. and see into their spirit, BY THE SPIRIT! The KJV says it like this, "Wherefore henceforth know we no man after the flesh..."

The word "know" in Greek means "to see, to experience, to know, to perceive, to have regard for, to pay attention to." God is telling us that IS indeed possible. In fact, by His love you can come to a place where you do not live according to the behaviors of those around you. Instead you pay no attention to anything but His love when you deal with others.

The enemy will try to get you to play checkers with people, meaning, they make a move, you make a move, they throw darts, you throw darts, they respond in anger, your respond in anger. But God has given you a mind to play chess. He has given you a strategy that is far beyond playing tit-for-tat with others. I don't have to wait to see how someone responds to make up my mind how I feel about a situation. My actions and feelings are not dependent on others, but rather on Christ. I do not want to get tangled up in the heat of a moment or give in to emotions and live reactionary, but instead I want to be driven only by His love. This is pleasing to God.

"No one engaged in warfare entangles himself with the affairs of this life, that he may please him who enlisted him as a soldier."
2 Timothy 2:4

This is not a command from God, but an empowerment of God. The choice you have to operate from His Spirit and mirror His Spirit in every situation within every relationship is not a guilt trip, it is a gift! Remember, where His Spirit is, there is freedom and knowing you have the ability to choose how you want to respond, instead of living in reaction, is liberating. By doing so, you will indeed enforce a change in the pattern of your relationships. This is not dependent on the other party; it is solely dependent on your ability to mirror God and His nature.

WHERE'S THE OFFENSE?

One of the things that will quickly derail you from changing the pattern is offense. I strongly believe that being offended is one of the ways that Satan keeps us from mirroring the Holy Spirit. Enforcing change should never be motivated by personal offense, but rather because you recognize that God's design has been offended. I love the story of Jesus overturning tables in the temple because it reveals how seriously Jesus took God's design for the temple.

"Then Jesus went into the temple of God and drove out all those who bought and sold in the temple, and overturned the tables of the money changers and the seats of those who sold doves. And He said to them, "It is written, 'My house shall be called a house of prayer,' but you have made it a 'den of thieves.'" Matthew 21:12-13

Jesus didn't respond out of personal offense, but out of offense of the design. He had nothing to gain or lose by His actions. In other words, He wasn't fighting for Himself. He fought for God's intention for the temple. God had a design in mind for the temple and it was for holiness, purity, and prayer, and Jesus enforced that design.

Believers house God's Presence within us, making us the temple of Christ. And just as Jesus responded when the design for the temple was offended, when our design is not being "treated" according to God's design, there should be a righteous anger within us that says, "This is not OK!" And it is not OK because it is not God's design. But it cannot have anything to do with what we do or don't deserve, but only with what He desires for us in relationships. We cannot afford to pick up a personal offense.

Personal offense stirs up the soul, while remembering His design will stir up the spirit. This mentality will navigate your motive and ensure that you have what is best for both parties in mind and not just yourself. If what you have in mind lines up with what God has in mind, then your only motive will be to fight for His design instead of just fighting for yourself.

YOUR EMPOWERMENT

You can only enforce change from your end. You cannot control how another person does or does not respond. By keeping your motive set on God's heart instead of your own personal offense, you will find yourself free to extend grace when you don't see the change you want.

"If it is possible, as much as depends on you, live peaceably with all men." Romans 12:18

I use this verse to remind my clients that God has called us to do our part, but we cannot control the part of others. However, not seeing change in the other party does not give you the right to give up pursuit of His design from your end. Remember, your motive is not to get results; your motive is to honor God and His design. This means you are only concerned with how God is responding to your choices and actions.

YOUR HOPE

The choices you make will not always be popular with man, but if the Spirit leads them and the motive is pure, they will be powerful. This is the hope that we have, not that our actions will change others, but that we ourselves will be changed as we shift our own hearts and mirror Jesus in our relationships. The only hope that won't disappoint is a hope set on Christ. If you are hoping that your actions will change others, then you will likely experience disappointment, plus your motive is not set right. But, if you do what you do motivated by God's heart, then you will experience a satisfaction that doesn't come from any person, but rather comes from God. I promise, this will never disappoint!

"Therefore, having been justified by faith, we have peace with God through our Lord Jesus Christ, through whom also we have access by faith into this grace in which we stand, and rejoice in hope of the glory of God. And not only that, but we also glory in tribulations, knowing that tribulation produces perseverance; and perseverance, character; and character, hope. Now hope does not disappoint, because the love of God has been poured out in our hearts by the Holy Spirit, who was given to us." Romans 5:1-5

You see? If your heart and mind is set on His love for you, you will never be disappointed. God's love supersedes your expectations. You must be intentional to seek His affirmation and live to please Him alone. The knowledge that He allows every trial and tribulation to grow you up should cause you to press on; even when you don't see the results you want.

God is ever growing you and bringing you more into your God-design, which is the likeness of Jesus. He is not OK with you being halfway there. He allows challenges, which often come through relationships, to complete that design. Your hope should never be in *others* changing, but rather in the knowledge that He is changing *you*! So, when you are ready to make changes in your relationships, stay focused on what He is doing in you and refuse to believe the lie that there is no fruit in your efforts. You have the power to enforce change, but it starts in your own heart. This is the hope that Jesus promises that will not disappoint, and it is that hope that should be the motivating factor in redefining your relationships.

PRAYER PRACTICE

My hope is in You! My hope is in You! All other hope is false and I repent of looking to anything or anyone other than You to be my source of hope. I place my feet upon You, the Rock of my salvation, and I stand safely and securely on the solidarity of Your love. Thank You for being my One and Only, my First and my Last, My Sure Thing! Who else, what else do I need but You? You are my Rock, my Fortress, my Deliverer, my God, my Stronghold. May the words of my mouth and the meditation of my heart be acceptable in Your sight now and forever. (Psalms 18 &19).

In Jesus' name I pray, Amen.

Chapter 5
Setting Healthy Boundaries

Enforcing change may involve setting healthy boundaries. In fact, I would say that it will almost always require setting healthy boundaries. Learning to set healthy boundaries is necessary for establishing and maintaining God's design. It is how we communicate to others that we know who we are in Christ and that we respect His design for us. It is a form of self–respect that is based on confidence in your God-identity.

WHAT ARE HEALTHY BOUNDARIES?

Boundaries are limits we establish to protect our God-design from being offended. These limits can be physical, emotional, and/or mental "lines" that create a boundary that separates who we are and what we think and feel from the thoughts and feelings of others. We establish them to enforce who He created us to be and our individual personalities, desires and purposes.

To set personal boundaries is to honor and preserve your design and its uniqueness. It is how you take ownership and cultivate who you are in Christ. I believe that setting boundaries is what allows you to enjoy relationships to their fullest and experience true connection with others. They allow you to operate without fear of your design being offended or losing a sense of who you are and what you are designed for.

Before setting healthy boundaries, it is imperative that you remember that your enemy is not any person. Let's reflect back to Ephesians 6:12 for a moment.

"For we do not wrestle against flesh and blood, but against principalities, against powers, against the rulers of the darkness of this age, against spiritual hosts of wickedness in the heavenly

places."

Your goal in setting boundaries cannot be to come against the other party involved, or to "stick it to them" or "put them in their place." Your heart must be such that you are just as concerned for *their* design as you are for your own. To not set healthy boundaries not only offends your design, but it allows the other party to continue in their unhealthy patterns as well. Loving people is not always just "loving them where they are and accepting them the way they are." You must love them enough to confront that which is stealing their design. However the motive must be love and it must be done in love!

"Now the purpose of the commandment is love from a pure heart, from a good conscience, and from sincere faith." 1 Timothy 1:5

Every one of us has demons that we struggle with and that we allow to navigate our thoughts at times. Remember, I called these your strongholds. And strongholds cannot be dealt with according to the flesh; they are "pulled down" by the spirit.

"For though we walk in the flesh, we do not war according to the flesh. For the weapons of our warfare are not carnal but mighty in God for pulling down strongholds, casting down arguments and every high thing that exalts itself against the knowledge of God, bringing every thought into captivity to the obedience of Christ." 2 Corinthians 10:3-5

You must stay focused on this in order to operate out of the Spirit of God and in love when redefining patterns and setting healthy boundaries.

GOD'S BOUNDARIES

It is interesting that we are all quick to agree that God has placed boundaries in our lives with Him and what it looks like to walk in accordance to His Word, but that we often don't realize that He has also given us boundaries in the area of relationships.

These boundaries apply to every aspect of life, not just in your walk with Him, but also in your relationship with yourself and in your relationship with others.

I believe Psalm 16 to be one of the places where God talks about relationships, boundaries, and the importance of them. Let's take a look!

"Preserve me, O God, for in You I put my trust. O my soul, you have said to the Lord, 'You are my Lord, My goodness is nothing apart from You.'" (verses 1-2)

The word *preserve* used here in Hebrew means "to keep (within bounds), to guard, to protect, to restrain, to have charge of." The definition of the English word preserve means, "maintain something in its original or existing state." Some synonyms are *conserve, protect, maintain,* or *care for.* So what is the psalmist asking the Lord to preserve? "Me." Meaning himself, and the design for who he is created to be! The psalmist is relying on the Lord to direct him in maintaining his life and God's design for him. Moreover, he is placing his trust in God's design for him, not man's. He is declaring that God Himself is his source of "goodness" and were it not for God, he would not know what is even good. God is where we find our standard of measurement. He is the plumb line upon which we establish the integrity of our relationships and how they should be built. The psalmist recognizes that he cannot look to the world to define what will preserve his life or guard and maintain the "state" (design) that God established within him. Instead, he MUST look to God to teach him how to do that.

"As for the saints who are on the earth, They are the excellent ones, in whom is all my delight. Their sorrows shall be multiplied who hasten after another god; Their drink offerings of blood I will not offer, Nor take up their names on my lips." (verses 3-4)

The psalmist recognized the power to choose what kinds of relationships he will engage in. He states that the "saints" or those who live for God bring delight to his life, while those who chase down other gods bring him sorrow. He sees that the kinds of people he chooses to have a relationship with does indeed have an effect on his own life. I like to say it this way: Every relationship is either a liability or an asset to who you are and where you are going in life. In other words, relationships have the power to either grow you into your purpose or hinder you from your purpose. This connects back to many of the qualities of a healthy relationship—the idea of support and celebration, freedom and transparency. Being in relationship with people who respect your design and your purpose cultivates such qualities, there is no jealousy, but rather excitement and encouragement as you increase in who you are. There is ease in such relationships that releases refreshment and much delight! *The Message* says it like this, "And these God-chosen lives all around—what splendid friends they make!" Because of this understanding, the psalmist is able to confidently determine that he will NOT allow any relationship to interfere with who he is called to be and will not be taken by their ways or their devices, but rather stands on his identity in God. But remember, this decision flows out of his trust in God and his agreement with God's plan for him.

"O Lord, You are the portion of my inheritance and my cup; You maintain my lot." (verse 5)

Oh man, this is getting better and better! To say that God is the portion of your inheritance is to recognize that you understand that your natural "system" no longer defines you. Instead, all that you are and the choices and actions that you make are rooted in the person of Jesus Christ. He is your portion and His DNA is in you. The psalmist declares that the portion of God that is in him is the truth of who he is. He adds that God is also his cup, or his source of satisfaction. He is in essence saying to God, "All that I am, and all that I need is found in you." Not in any human. He then goes on to say, "You maintain my lot." Think about a lot, an actual lot that you would own. That lot would require maintenance in order for it to be groomed and kept. An unkempt lot is unsightly and will quickly get out of hand. This is also the case with the lot that we have been given from God; the design of Jesus in us and who He has called us to be. Even just one compromising relationship or one compromising action that does not uphold your God-design can be likened to not tending to a garden for even just a week. Yikes! How quickly unwanted weeds will begin to take root. At first it makes for an unattractive and chaotic-looking garden, but it wouldn't take long for those weeds to strangle out the roots of the plants, thus ultimately destroying the fruit. This is what I am talking about—the cutting off of our productivity and the fullness of who we are and our purpose when we allow others to compromise our "lot." Relationships will always pose to be helpful in maintaining your lot, but your lot maintenance is rooted in your walk with God! He alone maintains your lot! This means you must look to Him to establish your healthy boundaries. Unless your boundaries flow from His heart, they will not be pure. His lines fall in pleasant places.

"The lines have fallen to me in pleasant places; Yes, I have a good inheritance." (verse 6)

The psalmist acknowledges that with his lot comes lines. Again, think about an actual lot that you might own. That lot has boundaries, whether it is one acre or one hundred, what defines the lot is where the boundary lines are! Think outside the box with me about the beauty of boundaries. Consider a picture hanging on a wall without a frame; or walls without trim. We often pay more for a house that has crown molding bordering the top walls throughout the home. Why? Because it looks crisper, sharper, neater, and conveys a sense of order and cleanness. Without borders and boundaries, we would not know where one state ends and one begins. When you cross boundaries, the state laws change, as does the design for that state. Consider the same concept when it comes to what distinguishes countries. Your life is filled with lines—boundaries that are created to bring a sense of order and to distinguish the picture from the wall or one state from another. The same is true for your design—it comes with boundary lines, and God puts them in pleasant places. The Hebrew word for pleasant means "delightful, sweet, lovely and agreeable." Some of us need to hear that! While much of the world will indeed bulk at your boundaries and will disagree with them, if they are God-made lines, then they will be sweet to your soul and though you may even not like them, your spirit will find them agreeable and fitting. We live in a world that disregards boundaries; people trespass on properties, and they trespass on lives, crossing lines and pushing the limits to satisfy the flesh. But just like putting a security system in your house, you must establish ways to enforce your personal lot!

"I will bless the Lord who has given me counsel; My heart also instructs me in the night seasons. I have set the Lord always before me; Because He is at my right hand I shall not be moved." (verses 7-8)

The psalmist is aware that God Himself has been faithful to counsel him, to guide him in wisdom and instruct him in ALL his ways. This includes your relationships. Oftentimes, we see people swing from no boundaries to fleshly boundaries. They respond in anger or hurt or fear or rejection and end up setting emotional boundaries that are not rooted in love and faith. Such boundaries will not be consistent since they are rooted in the fickleness of emotion and not in God's wisdom. This will be ineffective and is not God's design. Consider this truth found in James when seeking wisdom.

"If any of you lacks wisdom, let him ask of God, who gives to all liberally and without reproach, and it will be given to him. But let him ask in faith, with no doubting, for he who doubts is like a wave of the sea driven and tossed by the wind." James 1:5 & 6

The psalmist knows that wisdom that is from God will make him steadfast and stable. He stands upon the promise that God's counsel WILL be given "without reproach" and that is what he walks upon, thus he "shall not be moved."

When you recognize that God is who defines your design,

and determines what is OK and what is not OK within a relationship, there will be a stubbornness that will cause you to fight; NOT FOR YOURSELF, but rather for the design. The knowledge that God is for you will make you immovable in your battle for a more excellent relationship. It cannot be about you, and it cannot be about the other party, it HAS to be only and always about God and His design! This is why it is great when both parties decide that together they want to partner in setting the boundaries needed to bring forth the most excellent design that God has in mind for their relationship.

"Therefore my heart is glad, and my glory rejoices; My flesh also will rest in hope. For You will not leave my soul in Sheol, Nor will You allow Your Holy One to see corruption." (verses 9-10)

Therefore? Therefore what? Therefore, since we have the confidence of God's presence and His love, we can rejoice; soul, spirit, AND body. My heart is glad, my glory rejoices, AND my flesh is at peace! I have literally seen people sick and diseased over years of walking in unhealthy relationships. The tension and the stress from operating in fear, or never saying no, or being cut down or belittled will indeed have its toll on the body. I see it every day in my counseling room. From friendships, to family connections, to marriages...the inability to enforce your design to be loved through healthy boundaries will break you down. The psalmist recognizes that walking in healthy relationships has been a key to his state of wholeness and health. We would do well to understand how much relationships impact our overall health and wellness! We must rest in the knowledge that God Himself is ever with us and is here to comfort and satisfy the needs of our soul. We need not fear man, because God will never abandon us...in life nor in death.

"You will show me the path of life; In Your presence is fullness of joy; At Your right hand are pleasures forevermore." (verse 11)

Finally, the psalmist is confident that God will continue to be everything he needs as he moves forward in life. He knows that God will navigate him into perfect places and relationships, and that it is God's presence that ultimately fills him up, not man's. Though there is pleasure to be gained in our relationships, there is no pleasure like that of God's presence and love. You can have all the relational pleasures in the world, but if you are not right with God, those pleasures will not last. Only through your own reconciliation with God and His love can you truly know the fullness of worldly relationships and the joy and satisfaction they can be.

Just for fun, I have added Psalm 16 from *The Voice*.

Protect me, God, for the only safety I know is found in the moments I seek You.
I told You, Eternal One, "You are my Lord, for the only good I know in this world is found in You alone."
The beauty of faith-filled people encompasses me. They are true, and my heart is thrilled beyond measure.
All the while the despair of many, who abandoned Your goodness for the empty promises of false gods, increases day by day. I refuse to pour out blood offerings, to utter their names from my lips.
You, Eternal One, are my sustenance and my life-giving cup. In that cup, You hold my future and my eternal riches.
My home is surrounded in beauty; You have gifted me with abundance and a rich legacy.
I will bless the Eternal, whose wise teaching orchestrates my days and centers my mind at night
He is ever present with me; at all times He goes before me. I will not live in fear or abandon my calling because He stands at my right hand.
This is a good life—my heart is glad, my soul is full of joy, and my body is at rest. Who could want for more?
You will not abandon me to experience death and the grave or leave me to rot alone.
Instead, You direct me on the path that leads to a beautiful life. As I walk with You, the pleasures are never-ending, and I

know true joy and contentment.

HULA HOOPS

I like to use a hula-hoop with my clients as a visual for healthy boundaries. I will stand inside of the hula-hoop and state that the area within the hoop represents me; everything about me. In it is my inheritance of Christ, my design. It is who I am, what I want, my desires, my needs, my plan, my purpose, my feelings, my thoughts, my opinions. It is me. My lot is within the hoop and my job is to cultivate myself with God through Jesus. When I groom and keep my own needs vertically, I get my need to love and to be loved, my need to connect and be heard, my need to be seen and noticed, my need for relationship, I get it all from God. Through my walk with Him, He teaches me what it looks like to "keep myself manicured." This means guarding my sleep, my time, my health, etc. and setting the priorities that many would say are selfish, but God would say are necessary!

The people around me have hula-hoops as well. Think about placing hoops on the floor that touch yours, but don't overlap. Although they are touching, there is space there for each person to maintain their own lot. There is a clear boundary that marks where I end, and that other person begins.

HOOP JUMPING

Too often, we get mixed up inside other people's lives. I like to call this "hoop jumping." We get sucked into their drama, or we just plain old butt-in where we shouldn't. There are two problems with this. First, you are taking on things that you are not designed to carry because they are not a part of your design. This can get muddy when it is with someone that we love. To be honest, women tend to struggle with this the most. We love to be martyrs so we spend our lives jumping into other people's hoops in order to try and "help them" and instead we end up overwhelmed and bearing more that we are designed for. Second, when we jump into someone else's hoop, we are abandoning our own. Think about it visually (if this were a video, I would be demonstrating it), to jump into another hoop leaves yours empty. When I listen to a client who is stressed or angry or overwhelmed by life saying things like, "Well, I had to go help so and so," or "I had to work the event," or "I needed to whatever," I respond by saying, "It sounds like you've been spending a lot of time in everyone else's hoops." I get out the hoops and move the client from hoop to hoop to demonstrate their hoop jumping. When they finally stop I point to their hoop and say, "Who's in your hoop?" "Who is manicuring your lot?" "Who is taking care of you?"

JOY INSIDE YOUR HOOP

We must get over this thinking that putting others first means abandoning our own hula-hoop. The minute I come out of my own inheritance that is found within my lot, I begin to operate from the soul. It will exhaust me and leave me feeling bitter and angry... typically at the person I am actually trying to help. There is no joy in operating outside of your hoop (remember Psalm 16). Your inability to say, "No" or set healthy boundaries will leave you feeling depleted and bitter.

I worked in the church nursery for years, even though I hated it. But I felt guilty since I had kids in there. Although it was never stated out loud, there was a subtle message that said as a mother, I needed to sacrifice one Sunday a month to serve the other mothers. Guess what? Every Sunday when it was my turn, I was fussy and came home irritated. It simply was not my gift and the bottom line is that I was not compelled to serve out of love, but rather out of guilt and fear. My fussiness was my own fault, and it was stemmed in my inability to simply say, "No." It was not good for me to serve out of the flesh, and it wasn't good for anyone around me either! Remember, there is a fullness of joy in staying within my God-design and keeping to His boundaries that have fallen in pleasant places.

EMPOWERING THE VICTIM

Setting healthy boundaries can be a difficult concept, especially for someone who is weak, timid, or operates in fear within a relationship. Now, it is important to note that not everyone who operates in fear has a legitimate reason for their fear. Sometimes the fear is simply perceived, or trained. Many live in fear of people in general, thus taking on a "victim mentality." For lack of a better term, we can call this person the "victim" of the relationship, meaning they are the underdog or the one whose design is being offended. Again, I do not call this out to victim-blame. My intention is not to call out a "victim" or to say it is their fault, but rather to call the "victim" up into the empowerment they have in Christ. With such people, it helps to remind them that their strength is not rooted in themselves, but rather in God. It is easier when we remember that we are not defending ourselves, but rather enforcing His design. It is His standard that we stand upon, not our own. That is where we find our courage to rise up.

When I am working with a victim, unless it is a case of physical abuse, I always try to teach them to set healthy boundaries. My first goal is to empower them! If I only counsel them to leave or abandon the relationship, they will likely just enter into another relationship that looks the same. That doesn't help them learn, but enables them as a victim. In fact, it is typical that most of them have had multiple relationships where they are the "victim." Although I truly believe that emotional abuse is just as damaging as physical abuse, I am not talking about physical abuse. They should be approached differently. While my first goal in emotional abuse is to equip and empower the victim, in cases of physical abuse, I counsel the victim to get away to a safe place. I want to be clear in making that distinction. In cases of emotional abuse, setting boundaries and having consequences when those boundaries are crossed takes a lot of courage. Those boundaries will either better the relationship, or they will shatter it. It is a risk, but the alternative is foregoing God's design. Either way the risk is worth it because ultimately joy and life is found in enforcing His inheritance for you. I have personally experienced both responses (some improved, some shattered) in some of my own relationships. But in each case, I was unwilling to allow the personality of the relationship to stay unhealthy, and I was unwilling to allow God's design for me to be offended any longer. It was not only squelching His fullness of joy in my life, it was also negatively impacting my physical health, my emotional/mental health, and my spiritual health. This is not at all in line with Psalm 16!

WITH WHOM DO I SET BOUNDARIES?

It is important to state that we should not walk around setting boundaries with every person we encounter or even are in some way connected with. Discernment and wisdom needs to be practiced. But ultimately, you have to decide if the relationship is "worth" fighting for in God's eyes. This question should definitely involve the Lord to ensure that you don't answer out of your own flesh. It would be easy to dismiss setting healthy boundaries out of fear of how it might "shake things up." But it would be equally as easy to use the concept of setting healthy boundaries to simply get what you want or to "force your ways and wants." You should pray about when and if it is appropriate to set healthy boundaries in each encounter and relationship.

CONSEQUENCES

Just like in real life, crossing boundaries has consequences. If I set boundaries in my diet, but then cross those boundaries, there will be consequences. If I party through school and don't set boundaries in my schedule to get my work done, there will be a consequence reflected in my grades. Consequences are God's natural way of teaching us and molding us into wisdom. In our housing program, we help the ladies, but we never interfere with natural consequences; they are a part of life's teacher! Therefore, it is important that when you decide to set boundaries that you have a consequence in place for if and when that boundary may be crossed. This is healthy to remember for you, too. Any time you are trying to change a pattern, it helps if there is a communicated consequence that will demonstrate that you are not just blowing words into the air, but that you mean business. It is one thing to set boundaries, it is another to enforce them. This can be as simple as saying, "When you speak to me with a condescending tone, I will be stopping the conversation until you can adjust your tone." That is a healthy boundary (and one that is pleasing to God) and there is a consequence. What you are saying is, "If you want the pleasure of connecting with me, then I am going to enforce that you speak to me in love as God would want." The beauty of this is that it not only protects your design, but it also teaches the other person how to function in love. Remember, your motive should be love, not anger.

All consequences should be firm but loving. Although both parties may not like the consequence (of course they won't), there should be safety and a sense of sound-mindedness that is communicated through the consequence. There is solace in knowing that one of you in the relationship is no longer being reactive but rather has thought out how important a boundary is to the point of holding that boundary in place. Remember your motive is love and a desire to deepen connection.

For the sake of offering another very practical example, let me talk to you for a minute about sarcasm. Many people are raised in a system that embraces and practices sarcasm as a way of humor. In fact, our culture in general accepts sarcasm. The problem with most forms of sarcasm is that there are hints of truth masqueraded in what is being said, and most often, they are being said at the expense of another person. Sarcastic comments can be passive-aggressive, cowardice ways of seeping what you are really feeling. Comments often come off degrading and belittling the person to whom they are directed. This can leave that person feeling like they have no choice but to either take it or defend themselves. They often come back with more sarcasm, thus the mirroring spirits begins. The first few years of my marriage, Brad would often play sarcastically with me; it was a part of his culture, especially as an athlete. However, I was not his teammate, I was his wife, and frankly I lacked the security to know how to handle it. Not knowing what to think, and having a sharp tongue at the time, I would often snap back at him in defense and with the same level of sarcasm. This often led to a series of sharp comments that ended up leaving me feeling unloved and Brad disrespected. Eventually, because I was being told that I just needed to "be quiet and pray about it," I ended up just being quiet and taking the verbal jabs. This only shut down communication and there was a loss of connection. I didn't feel as though Brad understood how I felt and I didn't know how to communicate that to him. This led to my feeling backed into a corner and stripped down during times of "playful banter," and I could do nothing about it. Now, let me be clear here; this end result was not Brad's fault, as a couple we developed this pattern together. My insecurity kept me from knowing how to respond; I swung from defense to disconnect, but neither response was godly!

To stop this pattern, I had to first reconcile my own wounds in my heart. I first had to believe the best and choose to believe that Brad's intent in his sarcasm was not to be hurtful, but playful. I had to shift from how I felt about it to how God felt about it. I settled in understanding that it was not the most excellent form of communication and that I did not understand how it was being used to build me up. Finally, one day IN LOVE, I told Brad how painful the sarcasm was to me. I told him that it felt as though I was being torn down instead of lifted up, whether or not that was his intent. During that time of our marriage, Brad was not very communicative about his love and feelings in general, so I was never sure how to take his sarcasm. I told him that I was going to point it out every time he used sarcasm and tell him that it was not OK to communicate his feelings and thoughts in that manner. At first, he responded defensively (as we all likely would) because he didn't realize the extent of it, and he saw nothing wrong with it. But as I started practicing that boundary, his pattern was illuminated to him and he began to see why it was so hard for my heart. You see, it was innately a part of Brad's behavior and he knew nothing different. There was no ill intent, however it did not cultivate connection and therefore was not God's BEST design for our communication. Brad certainly did not intend or want to wound me with his sarcasm, and we worked together to redefine that pattern.

I know this seems so simple and it isn't always that easy. In our case, the sarcasm was not meant with cruelty, but in many cases it is. Either way, a boundary should be set in any form of unhealthy communication. And remember, if it isn't God's most excellent design, then it isn't healthy. Sarcasm is just one of many examples that I could give in regard to types of unloving communication that tears one another down. Just like Brad, I had my own forms of communication that were not building him up... like silence. My shutting down and saying nothing communicated disdain, disapproval, and rejection. It was a disconnect that I used to let him know I wasn't happy. Come on ladies, you know what I am saying! Yet, this is the accepted pattern in many relationships, not just marriages. And too often we make excuses for that behavior when it is not God's best design. Brad and I had to come together to work to change that pattern. It was not my intent to hurt him, but rather I was just trying to "be heard." But, the result was that he was wounded and that was not OK. As he began to point it out and remind me that this was not OK, I started to change my pattern.

In both cases, instead of putting up with the behavior, one of us chose to change our response first. This change of response enforced a change in the other's behavior. In other words, we changed the way our individual gears spun, thus causing a change in the entire machine. The pattern was altered!

WHEN DO I PRACTICE CONSEQUENCES?

Knowing there are consequences helps you think ahead of time about how an unhealthy pattern offends God; those are the only things you should "hold the line on." This is not about what you think you deserve or what you want, or what offends you or makes you mad... it is about God's design and what offends HIM! I cannot stress this enough. This book is not written to give you permission to defend yourself, it is written to empower you to uphold and enforce God's design for you AND those you are in relationship with. Only the things that you are confident are an offense to God's design should have consequences. Otherwise, you will be operating out of your soul and not His Word. This is not about getting what you want, but rather about enforcing what God wants for BOTH parties involved.

TWO PILLOWS, ONE BED

Let me sidetrack for a moment and touch on what I use to further demonstrate boundaries within a marriage. When we enter into a marriage, we become one flesh.

Yet, within that oneness, we each still have our own design. No one spouse should have their design dismissed for the other. God created marriage so that both can flourish together in their individual purposes and passions. It is like sleeping together in the same bed, yet having your own pillow. Brad and I sleep together every night. In fact, we sleep in a queen-sized bed. We are snugglers, so we often connect physically in the middle of the bed, but we do not sleep on the same pillow... there simply isn't enough room, and it would be uncomfortable. No one wants to share a pillow; it crowds your personal space! Now, let's be real for a moment. Obviously, there are times when we are on the same pillow for the purpose of intimacy. But this is intentional and mutual and it is to connect at a deeper level. This is the case with marriage as well. There are times when we mutually decide to "overlap" our designs, or lay one down for a unified purpose, however, it is not the norm, and it should work both ways.

For example, there are times when Brad will intentionally choose to sacrifice a desire or want that he has to connect with where my heart is in a particular situation. But he does not feel trapped by this or like he has to in order to keep me happy. He has freedom in that choice. Or sometimes, he will put his "head on my pillow" to protect me. He might make a decision that I don't necessarily want or agree with because he feels it is best. In such cases, I do not feel controlled, manipulated, or trapped by his head temporarily being on my pillow because I know it is not where he is going to remain. I do the same with him. There are times when I see he needs my help and I will put my "head on his pillow" to help, but not to enable him or control him. He knows this because it is not the norm. The norm is that we sleep in the same bed, but stay on our own pillows. And trust me, we both feel free to say, "Your head is on my pillow" when we feel our design is being offended by the other (wink, wink). I think you get the point. But again, the key is that both spouses respect that each of them was created with a kingdom design.

RESPECTING GOD'S DESIGN

Many people ask Brad how he feels about his wife being an ordained minister or preaching from a pulpit. Brad's response is always the same, "I love who God has called her to be and would never dare interfere with how HE is working in her and through her." He believes that to do so would be kicking against the goads. He has said that to take issue with it would be having contention with God, not me.

When we were first married, Brad coached a lot outside of his day job. I will be honest and tell you that I resented it for many years because I was jealous of the time he spent with all his players and struggled with feelings of rejection. But, I grew to understand that my issue was not with Brad, it was with God and what he was doing in Brad. Coaching is a part of God's design for Brad and he is very good at it. Although he no longer coaches on a court or a field, he absolutely still coaches within the business sect, which quite honestly sometimes still requires the same amount of time. However, because of my confidence in how God has designed Brad, I am able to support him and celebrate his successes.

Both of us have had to learn, and are still learning, how to set boundaries that allow us to pursue our passions while protecting our relationship, but ultimately, we trust God to navigate those boundaries in each of us. We have no fear communicating when we are feeling left out, left behind, rejected, unappreciated, not prioritized, forgotten, unloved, or whatever. However, we do not let those emotions become excuses for squelching each other's designs and purposes.

You must understand that God is working within both of you, and partner in the development of each other's designs. It is not one or the other... it is both of you together coming into your purposes and celebrating each other equally. No squelching, no jealousy, no boasting... just partnering, cherishing, and honoring HIS design for each of us! This is what it looks like to be one flesh, yet still be endowed with individual gifts, purposes, and passions that function separately and uniquely.

Look at it like you would the Trinity. Though the Trinity has three distinct parts, Father, Son and Holy Spirit, they still are One. And each of those three parts has their own purposes, functions, and designs... none is greater or more powerful than the other, but they are equally important to the Kingdom. This is how marriage is to be, two people bound by the Holy Spirit, each with their own purpose, function and design. Neither is greater nor more powerful, they are equally important to the Kingdom!

PRAYER PRACTICE

God, I thank You that You have given me a design for Your Kingdom and with it there is much purpose and intent. You have a plan for me, and plan to give me a hope and a future... plans that prosper and do not harm (Jer. 29:11). Your plan is good and it fits me. I thank You for the wisdom that You give to help me discern what is of Your design and what is not. I pray that my eyes of understanding would be enlightened that I may know the hope of YOUR calling (Eph. 1:18).

In Jesus' name I pray, Amen.

Interlude

OK, so we made it through the "workshop" portion of the book. It was important to have a general understanding of types of relationships and how relationships work so that you can fairly assess where you are in your own relationships. One of the greatest things that will keep you from experiencing God's best in any area of your life is lack of knowledge. Hosea reminds us how lack of knowledge can actually bring about destruction.

"My people are destroyed for lack of knowledge..."
Hosea 4:6

This word "knowledge" comes from the Hebrew word "yada" which includes the idea of knowing, perceiving, discerning, finding out, to be acquainted with, to be instructed, to recognize or to know by experience. We must become acquainted with and learn to recognize signs of health within relationships. Otherwise, we may find ourselves settling on one that is less than God's very best.

In the first section, not only did I feel it was important to help you assess your current relationships, I wanted to empower you with some practical tools. However, as I stated, Section 1 without Section 2 would be incomplete. In fact, the key to successfully implementing the ideas in Section 1 is rooted in this next section! This is why I consider Section 2 the meat of this book.

Perhaps now your eyes have been opened to see any unhealthy patterns in your current relationships and you are ready to receive the heart of the matter, which is the necessity to be reconciled with God first and being reconciled with yourself second. Once these two are in order, you can walk in reconciliation with others, establishing healthy relationships and entering into the "love cycle" of loving and being loved.

Section 2

Establishing Healthy Relationships:
To Love and To Be Loved

Chapter 6
God's Pattern for Relationships

The majority of this book so far has involved considering your relationships with others, which typically is the focus when learning about establishing healthy relationships. It makes perfect sense, right? I mean, we live a life with people all around us and it is what we struggle with the most. I often say that relationships are the best and worst part of life. Remember the Muppets and that song they sang about women? "You can't live with them and you can't live without them?" I think we could sing that song about a lot of our relationships, don't you? So, of course we have to spend time discussing the logistics of relationships with people, after all, that's our goal, right? To establish healthy relationships and to live a life loving and being loved, hence the name of this book!

What you may not realize is that your relationships with others are greatly impacted by your relationship with God and the relationship you have with yourself. This is why this second section of this book is imperative. If you don't realize that the root of relational brokenness is in your own walk with God and agreeing with who He created you to be, you will struggle in the way you relate to others.

If I had to seek a pattern that God gives for establishing healthy relationships, I would say it is found in the greatest commandment. And while I am not really a "life is a pattern" girl, I do think this commandment clearly states that there are three relationships in life: One with God, one with self, and one with others. Furthermore, I believe this commandment shows how each of these relationships correlate and affect the other ones.

"Teacher, which is the great commandment in the law?" Jesus said

to him, "'You shall love the Lord your God with all your heart, with all your soul, and with all your mind.' This is the first and great commandment. And the second is like it: 'You shall love your neighbor as yourself. On these two commandments hang all the Law and the Prophets." Matthew 22:36-40

Not only is there a correlative pattern in this commandment, we hear Jesus state this as the Great Commandment. He stressed the importance of healthy connections. In fact, He says the whole law was summed up in this one statement. In other words, Jesus emphasized that at the core of walking in His ways was love and healthy connections! That being said, I think we can learn a lot about how to connect in a healthy manner through what is said in this passage.

This section has 3 parts: God-Reconciliation, Self-Reconciliation, and Reconciliation with Others. Here are nuggets of what you will learn in each part.

Part 1: GOD

"You shall love the Lord your God with all your heart, with all your soul, and with all your mind."

Experiencing your own love relationship with God must come first as you work toward healthy relationships with others. It is so important to be reconciled with God in every area of your life. If you are out of alignment with God and what He says, everything else will be out of sorts. Your mindset about God affects how you see yourself and therefore how you see others. Without the firm foundation of His love, you will never come into the perfect design of loving or being loved.

Part 2: SELF

*"You shall love your neighbor **as yourself.**" (Emphasis mine)*

OK, this is where we often skip something very important.

Typically we hear, "Love God, love others." But what about loving yourself? This portion of the commandment specifically mentions how you love yourself and the affect that it has on how you love others. It indicates that when we love ourselves, we will love others.

"You shall love your neighbor AS you love yourself." Think about how we would receive it if we said, "AS you love yourself, you shall love your neighbor." We must embrace the concept of self-love, not in a worldly sense, but in a godly sense: not out of your flesh, but out of the Spirit. We know how to love ourselves from the flesh, which is why Jesus uses that comparison, but instead of squelching that self-love, you must learn how to line it up with God's love and design.

It is important to practice ministry to self. Scripture is clear in many places that we will only be able to minister out of what we have first received...and that often our ministry to others is actually rooted in our own healing. In other words, our self-reconciliation navigates how we reconcile with others. Here are some verses that communicate this concept.

"And be kind to one another, tenderhearted, forgiving one another, even as God in Christ forgave you." Ephesians 4:32

"Heal the sick, raise the dead, cleanse those who have leprosy, drive out demons. Freely you have received; freely give." Matthew 10:8

"Praise be to the God and Father of our Lord Jesus Christ, the Father of compassion and the God of all comfort, who comforts us in all our troubles, so that we can comfort those in any trouble with the comfort we ourselves receive from God." 2 Corinthians 1:3-4

"The things which you learned and received and heard and saw in me, these do, and the God of peace will be with you." Philippians 4:9

Skipping the importance of self-reconciliation and the importance of loving who you are and the fullness of your creation has great effects on how you will connect with others around you. Falling short on the ministry to yourself first and on self-love will decrease your love for others.

Part 3: OTHERS

"You shall love your neighbor as yourself."

This brings us to reconciliation with others. Although we spent a lot of time discussing our horizontal relationships in Section 1, we will circle back around to it at the end of this section. After focusing on God and self, you will see how your relationships with others are affected. I hope you will find that all of the emotional challenges you face in relationships are typically rooted in your own relationship with God and yourself. This gives you much authority in how you respond to those around you and the challenges you face.

Now you've seen the pattern for the duration of this book. I warn you that you may get your toes stepped on. It is so much easier to sit in a place of blaming others for relational hardships, than to look up or in the mirror. However, looking at your own walk with God and how you love yourself puts you in the driver's seat of your relationships with others. It keeps you from falling prey or becoming victimized.

Jesus's relationship with others was not based on how those people acted, it was based on God's love for Him and confidence in who He was and love for His purpose. Think about Judas and his betrayal, or the three disciples who were in His inner circle who fell asleep on Him in His greatest hour of need, or Peter's denial of Him three times. Those circumstances were inconsequential to Jesus because He loved God and loved Himself; meaning He was in love with His design, His purpose, and His calling. Out of those two loves, He was able to love others!

Part 1
God

Chapter 7
God's Love for Us

Intimacy never involves just one person. Just as the old adage goes, "It takes two to tango," God has gone to great lengths to dance with mankind. From the time He walked with Adam and Eve in the Garden of Eden to this day, His desire has not changed. Over and over God draws mankind into intimacy, wooing us into His reconciliation through the blood of Jesus. Knowing that this is God's ultimate desire, and because Jesus emphasizes our intimacy with the Lord in the great commandment, we are going to start with our love relationship with God and how to be reconciled with Him. Intimacy starts with reconciliation.

TO BE RECONCILED

According to Webster, the word "reconcile" means *to restore friendship or harmony, to settle or resolve, to make consistent or congruous or to cause to submit or accept something*. In Greek, it means the business of money-changers, exchanging equivalent values, the adjustment of a difference, and the restoration to favor. I like to say that reconciliation means to be brought together or to be in total alignment. So if I were to lay myself onto the blueprints of God, I would line up with His heart and character.

Now before I go on, I need to point out that many people assume that they are walking in reconciliation with God simply because they are saved. It is possible to be saved, and yet still have many things that are not reconciled with God. This happens when a believer is not in congruency with the mind and heart of Christ. It is possible to receive the Divine exchange of your sin for His righteousness through His blood, yet not be in submission to it or accept the fullness of His favor. When you have areas in your thinking or feeling that are not harmonious with what God tells you, those things are not reconciled.

I can have all the knowledge of who God is and what He says, but if it is not my reality, then there are things not reconciled within me. I can even know the right Scriptures, but if they are not fleshed out in my life, then I am not walking in reconciliation.

Examples:

- Walking in fear or worry instead of the reconciliation of His peace even though I know that God says, "...be anxious for nothing..." (Philippians 4:6)

- Walking in depression instead of the reconciliation of His joy even though I know that God says He's given me "beauty for ashes and the oil of joy for mourning...the garment of praise for the spirit of despair." (Isaiah 61:3)

- Walking in judgment or criticizing others, instead of the reconciliation of His unconditional love that always believes the best. (1 Corinthians 13)

You see, I can have knowledge but still live disconnected. While this is common, it shouldn't be accepted as normal. At some point, we need to recognize that it is not the fullness that God has intended for us as His children. This lack of reconciliation is what I call being at enmity with God or being at odds with His Truth. It is being out of alignment with Him. This lack of reconciliation will allow room for the enemy to play in your life...and you don't want that! Any place where you are not one with God and who He is creates a "gap" in your soul. Now hear me when I say that nothing separates you from the love of God (Romans 8:38-39), however, you allow gaps when your heart and mind are not adhering to God's ways.

I am not saying this to condemn you, but rather to inspire you. I want you to be vexed by the places in your heart and mind that are not in harmony with God! You have to recognize the loss of not being reconciled fully with His favor and desire to be rid of anything misaligned. Before you can pursue complete reconciliation with God, you need to acknowledge that there are likely places you have not reconciled.

PRAYER PRACTICE

God, I thank you that by Your blood, I have been brought back into oneness with You. You have restored me and redeemed me and have put into me the fullness of who You are through the Holy Spirit. I realize that I often don't line up with You. Too many times, my heart and mind are at war with You and that tension and strife rises up within me because of it. I ask You to cleanse my mind completely. Purge my heart of anything that does not look like You. Drag my soul into alignment with You, Father, that I may walk reconciled with Your heart and Your Truth. I thank You, Daddy, that You have brought me this far and I trust You to complete what You have started!

In Jesus' name I pray, Amen.

WHERE DO WE START?

How do we walk in reconciliation with God; in a healthy relationship with Him that is filled with intimacy? Where there is no difference between us, but rather we are one? He is in me and I am in Him and there is no spot where He ends and I begin but rather we are synchronized and in total harmony? I think this is what it means to be hidden in Christ.

"Set your mind on things above, not on things on the earth. For you died, and your life is hidden with Christ in God." Colossians 3:2-3

What does it look like to be so set on God that you become hidden in Christ? I think it is possible that is what was happening with Enoch when the Bible says that he walked with God until he was no more (Genesis 5:24). Is it possible to "Enoch" to the place where we are no more? To die to yourself to the point where you are no longer seen, but only Christ is seen through you? Isn't this the point of living for God? Paul said it like this:

"I have been crucified with Christ; it is no longer I who live, but Christ lives in me..." Galatians 3:30

Reconciliation requires death of self. It means that I am going to submit my flesh and all its thoughts and desires to be lined up with God—body, soul, and spirit. You must start by surrendering to God and His nature of love to walk in reconciliation.

AGREEING WITH HIS LOVE

Let me reflect back on the idea that God woos us in to submission. He does not command His love on us or force it, nor does He force us to agree with it. Instead He draws us into a place where we melt into His arms and willfully lay all things at His feet.

"We love because He first loved us." 1 John 4:19

"John also tells us, 'in this is love, not that we loved God but that he loved us and sent his Son to be the atoning sacrifice for our sins.'"
1 John 4:10

Clearly, it was God's desire and plan to establish a relationship between mankind and Himself. And while a relationship with God does indeed require a love exchange, I want to stress the importance of receiving His love before you can return it. A healthy relationship with God starts with believing and receiving His love. You must agree with the love He has for you! If you know me or have heard my sermons or have read any of my books, you will hear this truth spoken over and over. I say it continuously and I teach it continuously. My clients probably get tired of me talking about the importance of believing and receiving His love. I start my own intimacy with God every day by stating that I believe His love and receive it.

PRAYER PRACTICE

Father, thank You that Your Word tells me that You first loved me; that You initiated our relationship by Your love. I thank You that You drew me to respond to Your love. I believe that Your love for me is unconditional, and that I am worthy of that love. I believe that Your love is available and I wallow in that love. I believe that Your love is forever being poured out upon me and in me, and I receive it to the point of overflow. You are the essence of love and You cannot be anything less towards me. I rebuke any thought that would resist and challenge Your love. I shift my full self into total agreement with Your love and what that looks like for me. Thank You, God!

In Jesus' name I pray, Amen.

Religion will often tradition us into something that looks like love for God, but the truth is that God Himself woos us into loving Him as we come to know His love first. After all, if we don't know His love, then what do we really know about love at all? At best, we will muster up what we think love is supposed to look like. In such cases, the world, the church, our past, our feelings, or our thoughts become your frame of reference for how you love. God should be your frame of reference. It is through receiving God's love that you learn what true love really looks like, and frankly what true love is meant to feel like.

Remember the woman at the well? Jesus met her where she was, and there was no demand on her to love Him, but rather out of His love and kindness toward her, she was swooned! She was won over by His love. We could even say that He "romanced" her. That's right, God is romantic!

It was this "romance" that caused so many to follow Him. It was His character and nature of love. Crowds followed Him wherever He went. He couldn't escape them; they were awed and swooned by His ways. Nowhere in the gospels do we see an example of Jesus demanding a following. He invited, but most were drawn to follow Him because of His love.

"The Lord appeared to us in the past, saying; 'I have loved you with an everlasting love; I have drawn you with unfailing kindness.'"
Jeremiah 31:3

"No one can come to me unless the Father who sent me draws them." John 6:44

It is interesting to note that the word "draw" here denotes the idea of drawing from the inside. God appeals to the heart, He works from the inside out, and we see this in the life of Jesus. He was very good at pursuing intimacy with people. Just like the Father, He desired connection with everyone, and this is the desire that is within us as His creation as well.

DESIGNED TO BE LOVED

This is how we begin to come into the fullness of our design. It is not about deserving to be loved, it is about our design to be loved. I agree with God, I am designed for love. Why? Because He wants me to be the object of His love. He designed me to be loved so that He could be my Lover! This is what motivates God to draw us to Him. It is not so that we would be His submissive servants, but rather that we would be His Beloved. Do you agree? Will you let Him love you? Instead of living a life that says, "I love you, God," will you live a life that says, "I love you too, God"? Do you see the difference? One starts with me and what I am going to do for God. It is about my affection, my devotion, and my commitment to Him. But the other starts with God, and what He has done for me. It is about His affection, His devotion, and His covenant of love with me.

Our tango with God starts with Him. He initiated it from the beginning of time and He is ever inviting us to take the dance floor with Him. Reconciliation starts by simply letting Him lead. Surrender to His footsteps and receive His love. You don't have to do or be anything but you, so relax and receive. There is freedom on His dance floor!

88

THE FOUNDATION OF HIS LOVE

You must know our worth of His love and choose to believe it. Until you are reconciled with His love, you will continue to struggle with feeling rejected and unloved by mankind. You will have fears and insecurities in your relationships and will be navigated by everything except God's love. It is only through knowing His love first that you can even begin to grow in the confidence of your design and the worth of your design. This is foundational when establishing healthy relationships. There is no other love like His and when His love is your satisfaction, suddenly every other relationship comes into His perspective.

PRAYER PRACTICE

God, what an incredible dancer You are. I thank You for taking my hand and lovingly leading me about the dance of life. I surrender to Your lead and I trust that You will lead in love. Teach me Your love that I would know it and my life would be built upon it. I am drawn by Your ways and enamored with Your heart. Thank You for teaching me to be in step with You. May we dance as one all the days of my life!

In Jesus' name I pray, Amen.

Chapter 8
Bring Back the Honeymoon

Now that you know that your love relationship with God starts with believing and receiving His love first, let's move on to learning more about what it looks like to live in response to that love. How do we intentionally stir up or focus on nurturing our love relationship with Him? I know this sounds elementary, but I think too often we get into a "rut" with God and we lose our fervor or the "freshness" of our relationship. The "romance" gets lost.

Isn't this true of marriages as well? In the beginning we refer to the excitement and passion of marriage as "the honeymoon phase" and somewhere along the road of life, the relationship loses that. It is sad that society considers that normal; it has become acceptable to lose passion in marriage.

MY MARRIAGE

Part of what triggered this whole message was the loss of that passion in my own marriage. Brad and I were rounding the corner to 25 years of marriage. We had 6 children and for the most part, we "got along" just fine. But in the midst of that, I began to feel as though our marriage had become rote and even a bit stale. We no longer did the things you do as newlyweds...like calling each other to just say I love you, or buying each other "just because" gifts, or getting dressed up and going on dates, or showing a general affection toward each other. I was saddened by the fact that we hadn't held hands in what felt like years. Now, I want to be honest with you and share that I came to a point that I was very dissatisfied and fussy in my heart about my marriage. I felt unnoticed and not celebrated. Everything about our marriage was ordinary and expected, on both sides. We had settled into the familiarity of our rut that we had made over 24 years of marriage.

Remember, it takes two to tango, so it was both of us who played a part in establishing what had become a "passionless" personality in our marriage. We loved each other deeply, but took advantage of the familiarity and no longer worked to pursue and intentionally stir up our love. At the root of this, I felt deeply rejected and unloved. Being a counselor, I worked through that rejection internally with God, but I lacked the honesty and transparency that was needed to connect with Brad at a deeper level in this regard. I feared telling him that I was "unhappy" with the personality of our marriage and so I dealt with it by making excuses for the way it was. For example, both of us travel a lot for work and we would typically not interact while we were apart. When the kids were little, Brad knew I was busy and tired at nights and during the day, he was working so I didn't want to interrupt him. Thus the pattern developed. And even when those reasons were no longer the case, the routine of our travel times was already established. When people asked if I had heard from Brad, or vice versa, we would just say something like, "No, we typically don't talk when we are out of town." It was our normal and we assumed that since that's the way it had always been, that's just the way we would continue. Lo and behold, that is not what either one of us preferred, but neither of us had bothered to communicate that.

I realized that I needed to open this up to Brad and ask if he was willing to discuss patterns that we had developed that we didn't really like. I kept in mind the power we had to change and redefine the gridlines of our marriage. There were many ways that both of us had even become ignorantly neglectful and apathetic toward each other and our marriage as an institution. We were not stirring the flame, and the fire was going out! This was a slow process, but I realized how dull and disconnected my heart had become and it scared me. Here I was in ministry, counseling couples daily in their marriages, yet unsatisfied in my own. Again, there was nothing wrong with our marriage, but it lacked zeal. I felt as though I was simply a maid, secretary, mother to his children, and sex-mate. And he felt he was just a provider, handyman, father to my children, and a sex-mate as well. We had a functional marriage, but not a passionate one. This was not God's most excellent design and I knew it. I had to set aside my feelings and decide whether or not I was willing to fight; not for what I wanted, but rather for God's design for Brad and I.

It took much courage to approach the topic and at first it didn't go well. Brad, who also was struggling with rejection and fear on his end, simply heard me saying that I wasn't happy. Truth be told, I didn't approach the conversation the best way and looking back, I could have communicated my heart better. Nonetheless, my poor communication was better than no communication, which is what had been the case.

That day opened a can of worms, and we decided we would rather deal with them than let those worms rot our marriage. We agreed that we both felt God had something better in mind for us and that our mediocre marriage could indeed be "hot" once again. But it was going to require work on both our ends. It has since been a journey of falling in love again and reigniting the flames of our marriage. We chose not to fight for "our rights," but partner in fighting FOR God's design.

We've had to be intentional to support how each other feels when we communicate and not respond in defense. (It isn't always easy to mirror God's spirit when your flesh wants to mirror what is in front of you.) However, the alternative is shutting the other person down, thus breaking connection. This cannot be an option in marriage.

It took A LOT of transparency and courage to communicate how we were really feeling and what we really wanted from each other and in our marriage. That was extremely difficult and vulnerable after years of saying nothing. There was high risk of rejection and upsetting the apple cart every time one of us decided to be real with the other.

Learning to redefine patterns requires a lot of patience, especially since people tend to learn more from failures than successes. This is challenging enough when it is just yourself, but when it is two of you, the challenge increases. Brad and I had years of poor communication, false doctrines, hurts and wounds, and fearful patterns to overcome. We had to discuss what healthy communication would look like for us instead of what we had always been taught. And then, we had to practice those new forms of communication. We discovered that we had been given the authority to define what we wanted our marriage to look like, according to who we were and our personal designs...and that it wasn't too late to go after God's design for our marriage.

Brad and I now practice those honeymooning behaviors that we wanted all along. We have not settled for lukewarm, but rather intentionally do things to keep the fire stirred up between us. We romance each other, go on dates, buy each other gifts, celebrate each other's successes, freely communicate whatever is in our hearts, text each other sweet nothings and we talk every day when we are out of town. The fire of our marriage is burning hotter than the day we got married, which I am convinced should be the norm! Furthermore, we have determined to honeymoon for the rest of our years.

HONEYMOONING WITH GOD

There is so much more that I could say in regard to what Brad and I have learned and probably more will be sprinkled in this text, however, I don't want this book to be limited to marriage relationships. (Plus I am determined to write our story in a book of its own.) I share this story with you because it connects with the idea of honeymooning with God. Before you can experience intimacy in any relationship, you must be actively honeymooning with God!

Multiple verses in the Bible refer to Jesus as the Bridegroom and to us as the "Bride of Christ." This is an important frame of reference God uses to describe His intimate love for us. It is an indescribable love, but His best comparison is like that of a groom waiting for his bride on the day of their wedding. For many, it seems a distant dream to try and fathom living life in that moment of bliss, that honeymoon phase, yet that is exactly what God is after.

Take a moment to read this excerpt from my book *Mastering Your Seasons.*

"Therefore, behold, I will allure her, Will bring her into the wilderness, And speak comfort to her. I will give her her vineyards from there, And the Valley of Achor as a door of hope; She shall sing there, As in the days of her youth, As in the day when she came up from the land of Egypt. And it shall be, in that day," says the Lord, "That you will call Me 'My Husband,' And no longer call Me 'My Master.'"
Hosea 2:14-17

Recall I likened your winter season to that of a wilderness. A time when you are in a place of "nowhere" and experiencing a real dryness without direction. Look closely at this passage and see that God Himself is saying that He is "alluring" her into a wilderness. To allure means to entice or persuade. Why would God bring us into a place that the world and our flesh would consider miserable? That doesn't make sense to our human minds. In His infinite love, God may strip us down and isolate us in order to be alone with us and speak directly to us. He wants to intensify our intimacy and our reliance upon Him and Him alone. Read these verses paraphrased in The Voice:

"But once she has nothing, I'll be able to get through to her. I'll entice her and lead her out into the wilderness where we can be alone, and I'll speak right to her heart and try to win her back."

Wow! What a beautiful description of what is going on. The bigger picture of the heart of our situations and why God allows what He does.

God's desire is always to bring you into a greater understanding of His love for you and the depths of His passion. There is a shifting that He is forcing to come into play through this wilderness. A shift from looking at God as "Master" to "Husband." God is not content to have you view Him as a dictator or to be motivated in your work by fear of duty. He wants love to be your motive.

I couldn't have said it better myself. God is trying to get His Beloved to understand His desire to simply be her husband. He wants to reignite the fire and passion of their love and put a new song in her heart.

Much like my relationship with Brad, I fear that it is too common and considered normal to have stale seasons with God. While I am not disputing that we go through times that will challenge our passion, we should never consider lack of passion as a normal part of our walk with God. It is clearly not what we learn through Scripture. As I did in my marriage, I have had to overcome that lie. It is indeed possible for me to be walking through a wilderness or dry season spiritually, and yet still be passionate in my walk with God. This is much of what my book *Mastering Your Seasons* is about; remaining focused on the heart of God and His love during every season. It is possible to be in a season of dryness, yet be full of the Living Water!

> *"I will open rivers on the bare heights*
> *And springs in the midst of the valleys;*
> *I will make the wilderness a pool of water*
> *And the dry land fountains of water.*
> *"I will put the cedar in the wilderness,*
> *The acacia and the myrtle and the olive tree;*
> *I will place the juniper in the desert*
> *Together with the box tree and the cypress."*
> *Isaiah 41:18-19 (NASB)*

THE DEMONSTRATION OF LOVE

Part of what honeymooners are known for is their ridiculous display of love. They don't care where they are or who is around, they are affectionate and touchy and are likely to say things out loud that let others know how passionately they are in love. This was part of what Brad and I had lost over our years of marriage... the demonstration of love. It wasn't that we didn't love each other, because we did, we were apathetic in showing it. There was little to no expression of our love toward each other. If you remember in the beginning of this book, I said that one of the best ways to feel love is to express it. That being said, you can see where not only the lack of receiving a "demonstrated" love made us both feel unloved, but our lack of expression cultivated this lie as well.

I often say that the opposite of love is not hate; it is apathy. This is because love requires energy and time. Love without action is like faith without works (James 2). This does not mean the love does not exist; it just makes it ineffective. Just like faith without works is dead, love without action brings no life. In other words, there is no point to it. It is simply an emotion or feeling that unless expressed, no one knows even exists.

God knows that love requires action.

"But God demonstrates His own love toward us, in that while we were still sinners, Christ died for us." Romans 5:8

The Greek word for "demonstrates" means to *introduce, present, prove, show or establish*. It also includes the idea of placing things together or uniting parts into one whole. God's feeling of love is established or proved when the emotion is combined or united with action. The demonstration of love is what proves the truth of what we otherwise would not be sure of. How many times do we wait to see if a person's word is proved by their actions? Their word is established when it is united with the action of what they spoke. That's the proof in the pudding.

As Brad and I worked on intentionally demonstrating our love for one another, the lie that we were unloved was shattered between us. Our expression of love was the proof that left no room for doubt. We often hear the phrase, "You can't argue with facts," so when love is fervently expressed, the truth of that love is proven and the enemy's lies are diffused.

"And above all things have fervent love for one another, for "love will cover a multitude of sins." 1 Peter 4:8

Not only are the enemy's lies covered through demonstration; the lies in our own head are covered. This is part of what is meant by "a multitude of sins." It is not just the covering of another's sin, but also our own. Your fervency in demonstrating love guards your heart and mind like a cover wrapping you and protecting you from the enemy's attempts to destroy your relationships.

HIS STUBBORN LOVE

One thing I know, God's passion towards us never wavers. He is continually romancing us, pursuing us, celebrating us, sending us "sweet nothings" and He is ever communicating with us. His love is not conditional and is relentless. It is a stubborn love that is unwilling to let you go!

"Even if the mountains heave up from their anchors, and the hills quiver and shake, I will not desert you. You can rely on My enduring love; My covenant of peace will stand forever. So says the Eternal One, whose love won't give up on you." Isaiah 54:10, The Voice

"Hang my locket around your neck, wear my ring on your finger. Love is invincible facing danger and death. Passion laughs at the terrors of hell. The fire of love stops at nothing—it sweeps everything before it. Flood waters can't drown love, torrents of rain can't put it out. Love can't be bought, love can't be sold—it's not to be found in the marketplace."
Song of Songs 8:6-8, The Message

This is our example of love, and it is nothing like what the world would tell us. It is God's love that will keep us rooted in our true worth and reveal the fullness of our design. We must not settle for anything less than a honeymoon with God all the days of our lives.

❧ PRAYER PRACTICE

God I thank You for being the fire within me and that even when I try to ignore that fire, or when I don't tend to that fire, You still are burning for me. You never give up on me, but pursue

intimacy every moment of every day. With every sunrise I am reminded that You are My Holy Romance and that You are seeking me out. You desire to connect with me deeper every day and I respond Lord to Your calling of my heart. I thank You for stopping at nothing and that nothing can quench Your love for me. You burn for me, and I thank You for putting that burn in me. May I burn for You all the days of my life.

In Jesus' name I pray, Amen.

Chapter 9
Your First Love

Because we are created in God's image, we can be sure that just like He is a pursuer of love and romance, so are we. We get our passion from Him, and when that passion wanes, so do we. This is why it is so important that we learn to intentionally pursue God as our Lover and press into His heart more and more every day.

I was recently convicted by the passage in Revelation 2, where God addresses the church of Ephesus "affectionately" by calling them, "The Loveless Church."

"To the angel of the church of Ephesus write, 'These things says He who holds the seven stars in His right hand, who walks in the midst of the seven golden lampstands: "I know your works, your labor, your patience, and that you cannot bear those who are evil. And you have tested those who say they are apostles and are not, and have found them liars; and you have persevered and have patience, and have labored for My name's sake and have not become weary. Nevertheless I have this against you, that you have left your first love. Remember therefore from where you have fallen; repent and do the first works, or else I will come to you quickly and remove your lampstand from its place—unless you repent. But this you have, that you hate the deeds of the Nicolaitans, which I also hate.
"He who has an ear, let him hear what the Spirit says to the churches. To him who overcomes I will give to eat from the tree of life, which is in the midst of the Paradise of God.'" Revelation 2:1-7

I love the way this passage starts out with God pointing out all of the things that they are doing well. It is as if He is removing any opportunity for them to defend themselves by agreeing with the positives. I read the first part of this and think to myself, "Well, they are getting it right!" Works, labors, patience, intolerance for evil, testing the spirits, perseverance, patience AGAIN, labor AGAIN, not growing weary... these all sound great! In fact, I might even say this sounds much like the church today. I'll be honest and tell you that as I was reading this, I even felt myself nodding along as I ran through my own personal checklist. Works? Check. Laboring? Check. Patience? Check. But then the word "nevertheless" shows up! I know that when I was reading this, it was as if the spirit shifted into slow motion and the words were spoken very slowly with much emphasis. Each consonant was enunciated and I could swear the voice of the Holy Spirit turned into a bass instead of the gentle tenor voice I am accustomed to. I sensed that God was revealing to me that I was drifting from my first love. I wasn't sure exactly what this meant since my entire life is devoted to ministry. I mean, I spend most of my days working a ministry that houses those who are in need. We work daily to help them find their way back to wholeness by providing for them practically and teaching them biblical principles. I pray with my staff daily and lead a time of community praise and worship once a week. How am I drifting from my first love?! But, because I sensed His voice so strongly through this passage, I had to let the Holy Spirit search me.

Search me, O God, and know my heart;
Try me, and know my anxieties;
And see if there is any wicked way in me,
And lead me in the way everlasting. Psalm 139:23-24

The spirit of a man is the lamp of the Lord,
Searching all the inner depths of his heart. Proverbs 20:27

What came out of this was the Lord prompting me to ask myself these questions, "Is my ministry my first ministry, or is *God* my first ministry? And, is there a difference? Has my ministry become my first love, and if so, is that putting God first?"

I was confused by the common thought that ministry to God

looked like ministering to people. Isn't that what we are taught; that "our job" as believers is to minister to others? Is that what God says, or just what religion has decided for us?

RELIGIOUS WORKS

Going back to the passage in Revelation, God wasn't saying that He was unhappy with the church's lack of ministry engagement, or their "works." It wasn't that they didn't have works, but rather that their works were motivated by religion and were no longer based on the prompting of the Holy Spirit. Instead, they were based on tradition and routine. This led to a stale church filled with people who lacked the passion like that of being in love. The church was no longer flowing from the heart of God, but from rules and what they were told "church" was supposed to "look like." They were guided by precepts instead of by purpose, which is the letter of the law instead of the spirit of the law.

A church led by works and not by love is religious and rigid. Furthermore, the Bible says that works not compelled by the heart of God hold no power; there is no strength in them and they lack supernatural impact.

"For in Christ Jesus neither circumcision nor uncircumcision avails any thing, but faith working through love." Galatians 5:6

The Greek word for *avail* includes the idea of having force, ability, strength, or might. So, we can display works, do the right thing, follow the rules and traditions of religion, but if they are not flowing out of His love, they will hold no power. They will simply be mere activities.

OUR HOUSING PROGRAM

One of the challenges we have within our Crazy8 housing program is the need to have "rules." We must have them, yet we do not want to become religious with them, if you know what I mean. In fact, we don't call them rules, we call the list of standards our "covenant." They are simply things that we ask the ladies to agree

103

to when they enter into the program. Some will follow the covenant to the letter, while others will bend and even break the covenant. Neither case is following the spirit of the covenant. We don't want them to follow the covenant out of compliance or fear, but because they have bought into the beauty of the covenant and the standards that we feel emulate a healthy lifestyle. That is the spirit of the covenant; it is the purpose behind it. Conversely, those who bend or break the covenant also don't understand its purpose. However, there are those who truly have a heart to work their program yet sometimes don't get everything in their program accomplished the way "we think it should be done." This is where we, as a team, have the freedom to prioritize the heart intent over the outcome. Following the spirit of the covenant means that we understand the purpose behind it, and therefore we stay focused on the motive of each lady's heart. They set goals, but the purpose is to see growth as opposed to performance. We are not after perfection, but rather progression.

Therefore, the program has been designed to be like a fish tank. There is a general framework with clear objectives, but inside there is a lot of movement and freedom to flow. We must leave room for how the Holy Spirit is working individually in the lives of each lady with every situation. This requires a lot more work from our team than simply throwing the book or the rules at them when there are challenges. However, it also allows for a lot of creativity, which we love! It keeps us positioned near the Father in order to understand each of the residents and their hearts. After all, He is acquainted with all of their ways and has written every day ordained for them in a book (see Psalm 139). We MUST rely on Him to direct us in every situation, with each lady. We don't want the ladies to perform based on external rewards or consequences, but rather we want them to progress because of internal motivation and personal desire.

This is why we focus so much on pursuing the personal vision that God has put in each woman. The Bible says that without vision, we perish (Proverbs 29:18), so we can safely say that with vision, we thrive! Their purpose and plan is where we will find the movement of the Holy Spirit. And we don't want the ladies to perform based on external rewards or consequences, we want them to progress because of internal motivation and personal desire. This only comes by the Spirit of God.

The point here is that we have to instill a love in these ladies...for God first, and then for themselves and their own design. God has a plan for us all and when we fall in love with our purpose, we develop a passion for life! If all they do is religiously follow the rules without any heart behind it, then they will be no better off without the "whip at their backs" when they leave. And that would simply make our program no different than prison.

This is why our relationship with God and stirring up that first love is so important in life. Otherwise, everything you do is work-based which will wear you out and leave you feeling bitter and depleted.

MY LOSS OF LOVE

In all of this, I felt God asking me, "Lisa, am I still your first love?" I was very aware in this moment that much like my marriage, my walk with God had gotten very functional. It looked good and was filled with all the right actions, but my heart lacked passion. The spiritual romance was gone. The honeymoon was gone. Remember when you first came to know God and His love? Or those moments in your walk that you were passionate about Him and only Him...not about the work He had for you to do, or even necessarily about people, but JUST HIM? I wasn't feeling that anymore, and much like I felt in my marriage, I was not OK with it. I wanted the passion and the fire of not just loving God, but of being IN love with God. I wanted to honeymoon with God again! I refused to believe that just because I had been a believer for years meant that the excitement and passion of the love was over and to expect the passion of the honeymoon was unrealistic. I had learned that was not the case in my marriage, and I believed the same for my relationship with God.

FIRST

The word *first* in Greek includes the idea of *rank*. So I take this to mean, "Who or what is your *Number 1* love?" If you were to take a look at your life, your thoughts, your heart, your schedule, your finances, you would likely be able to rank areas of importance in your life. The question is, who or what would be first rank?

God is not OK with you living your life half-heartedly. He is a jealous God and He doesn't want to share you with the world. This includes your work within the world, even if it is ministry. There is no middle ground. There will always be a first rank in your life, and it is either God, or it is not. The devil will deceive you into compromise where you live a life half-in and half-out. Elijah the prophet said it best to the prophets of Baal:

"How long will you falter between two opinions? If the Lord is God, follow Him; but if Baal, follow Him." 1 Kings 18:21

Our world tolerates compromise. In fact, I believe we are encouraged to be tolerant to an unhealthy level. One of the worksheets that I do with my life-coaching and counseling clients is to make a list of the tolerances they allow in their lives. Then, they are to think about who they would be if they did not allow these tolerances. What they discover is that even small tolerances can alter who you are designed to be and the way you live. It is amazing to learn how many of us allow who we are to be compromised by what we allow or tolerate. Now, I realize that there is a healthy level of tolerance. We have to allow others to be free and not squelch their designs or their opinions. But I fear that too often, we tolerate to the point of squelching our own design in that process. To a fault, I think our culture has "shut up" the rights we have to our opinions and our feelings. We are no longer safe to speak up for what we believe for fear of being persecuted, or God forbid, shot to death. While I absolutely have my own strong beliefs and am appalled at how some may believe totally opposite of me, I will never think it is OK to keep others from expressing their beliefs. (I do think, however, that we could learn a thing or two about how to express ourselves tactfully, peacefully, and in love.)

My point here is that we too often give in to the ways of the world and compromise God's standards in the process. Although it is sad that we become ineffective for the kingdom in such cases, the real heartbreak is that we give up the potential of who we are designed to be in Christ. God is not OK with this. He is a jealous God, and He is not content to let us settle and waver between the world and His kingdom.

"Adulterers and adulteresses! Do you not know that friendship with the world is enmity with God? Whoever therefore wants to be a friend of the world makes himself an enemy of God. Or do you think that the Scripture says in vain, "The Spirit who dwells in us yearns jealously"?" James 4:4-5

Check it out in *The Message…*

"You're cheating on God. If all you want is your own way, flirting with the world every chance you get, you end up enemies of God and his way. And do you suppose God doesn't care? The proverb has it that "he's a fiercely jealous lover." And what he gives in love is far better than anything else you'll find."

God knows that to dance with the world is to give up your dance with Him. There is no in-between. The enemy will deceive you into thinking you can have both, or that little compromises or tolerances here or there won't hurt you. But the Bible is clear that we must diligently pursue God and His heart lest we drift away.

"Therefore we must give the more earnest heed to the things we have heard, lest we drift away." Hebrews 2:1

In Acts, there is mention of how the apostles continued "steadfastly" in the pursuit of God. (Acts 2:42) This means that just like within a marriage, we have to be intentional to stir up our connection with God and keep the kindle of love burning.

GOD'S JEALOUSY

God is not willing to compromise a child of His. He is jealous FOR you and He knows that the world will obscure the holiness of Christ in you. He will, therefore, continuously draw you back into His love. It is by His love that you are kept!

This is what the Father was doing with me when He challenged me through Revelation 2. He was expressing His jealousy for me. My heart had become distracted, and therefore divided, and my wholehearted devotion to God was no longer "wholehearted." There were other things that had first rank, namely, my ministry and the people that I was ministering to. It is possible—in fact, with mature believers it is more likely—that it will be "good things" that cause us to compromise our first love. In my case, it was my ministry. The Lord had my attention and I saw clearly that I needed to rekindle my First Love. I felt the jealousy of the Lord wooing me to remember Him and His love and drawing me to reposition Him into first place as my first love.

PRAYER PRACTICE

God, I thank You for being a jealous God and that You are not willing that anything would come between You and me. I am so thankful for the many times in my life that You have fought for me and wooed me back into Your arms. I realize that Your motive in drawing my affection to You is that You know that as I worship You, I will become more like You. Your ultimate desire is that I would live to my fullest and reflect Your glory! I declare You as my First Love and I speak against anything that would compromise my mind or my heart. I will not tolerate any wavering, but will remain steadfast in my pursuit of Your heart.

In Jesus' name I pray, Amen.

Chapter 10
Your First Work

After revealing to the church of Ephesus that they had moved away from their first love, God spoke this antidote...

"Remember therefore from where you have fallen; repent and do the first works..." Revelation 2:5a

It is important to realize that there is no one magic formula for dealing with everything in your relationship with God. That's part of the issue that is being attacked here...the danger of becoming religious or "algorithmic" in our relationship with God. A relationship should not function on rules and methods, but should flow heuristically. Scripture does suggest ways to walk in victory, however they are for the purpose of impressing the heart toward change. They are not for the purpose of mindlessly functioning under formulas and methods. So, as we move forward, let's keep these concepts in mind inspirationally and not dogmatically.

REMEMBER AND REPENT
Although I don't want to spend too much time on this part of the verse, I do feel it important to note the power of reflection. Recall the passage in Hosea where it says, "She shall sing there as in the days of her youth." God was taking "his beloved" back to a place of remembrance to reflect on all God had done for her and how his love had always been with her. The concept of remembrance is found throughout Scripture. In fact, I believe this was the purpose of traditions and why God put rituals in place for the children of Israel; to remind their hearts of who God was and all He had done. Altars were built for this purpose as well. They

were erected at a time and place of a significant movement of God that caused the "offering" of the people's lives. These altars served as a remembrance to the generations after them of what God had done and the total surrender of the people as a result. This is the power of remembrance.

Personally, when I am struggling in my own heart, I will intentionally spend time reflecting and recalling all of the ways I have seen God move in my life. Doing this reminds me of who God is and His goodness. This process tends to bring me to the revelation of places in my heart that are not in line with God and His love, which organically brings me to a place of repentance. Note that my repentance is inspired by His faithfulness and love.

The word repent means "to change one's mind." The process of intentionally reflecting and recalling God's goodness causes a shift in my thought process. It is "setting the mind on things above" (Colossians 3:2), and forcing a change, hence, "to change one's mind." Once the mind is changed, behavior typically changes as well.

I once heard a preacher teach on repentance through a story about a grandfather and his seven-year-old grandson. They were at some sort of fall festival when they came across a "haunted barn." The grandson wanted to go in, but the grandfather, knowing it would frighten the boy, told him that it was not a good idea. He warned him of all that would be in there, how it would scare him, and that ultimately he would not like the experience. Despite the counsel of the grandfather, the boy wanted to go anyway. The grandfather, not wanting to impede the boy's will, agreed to go with him. Once inside the haunted barn, things got dark really fast and the boy hung on more tightly to the grandfather's hand. Noises began, to thump and the floor began to rattle. They were only about a third of the way through when the boy looked up at the grandfather and said, "You were right; I am scared and I don't like this! I change my mind and want to leave." The boy had no sooner gotten those words out of his mouth when his body was turning around to change his direction. He did not keep walking forward through the barn, but instead turned and left. This is a picture of repentance. It is a change of mind that produces a change of direction. I would even throw in there that the change of mind includes a change of heart. This boy was not coerced into the new direction, but rather he was convinced into the new direction because his mind was changed. Ultimately he came into an alignment with the grandfather and gained the same perspective about his situation. This is what brought forth his change of direction.

This is what happens when we recall the goodness of God and we set our minds on things above. There is an inward change that produces a new direction. When your heart is aligned with God's, He will cause you to walk in His ways!

"I will put My Spirit within you and cause you to walk in My statutes, and you will keep My judgments and do them."
Ezekiel 36:27

DO THE FIRST WORKS

So let's shift into the statement: "Do the first works." What in the world does this even mean? If you remember, the Holy Spirit had stirred this whole passage within my own heart, and to hear Him saying to do the first works was a bit baffling to me. He had walked me through the lack of passion, and I had spent time reflecting and repenting for areas where my heart had drifted away and I had lost His fire within me. But these words, "do the first works" I was struggling with. Then, I recalled the advice that I had gotten from two different prophets when I first started the ministry.

One spoke: "Never get so busy ministering that you forget your ministry to God."

And the other spoke: "Always remember to minister to God first, and everything else will fall into place."

I wasn't sure what that had meant at the time, but God was bringing it back up and was using this passage to bring revelation to those words. Upon much prayer and study, here is what I learned.

THE PRIESTHOOD

Today, when we think of ministry, we think in terms of ministering to people. This is what we have been taught; that ministry involves serving and helping others. However, as I prayed more into what God was trying to reveal to me through this passage as well as the words of those prophets, He reminded me that I am of the "royal priesthood." (1 Peter 2) This led me to really look into the roles of priesthood in the Old Testament.

The term priest (*kohen*) is commonly used to refer to an official who was set apart from the rest of the community in order to carry out certain duties associated with worship and sacrifice. Look at the phrase, "Set apart from the rest of the community." This means that they spent their days NOT among people, but rather set apart. Secondly, note that their duties were associated with worship and sacrifice. This is very different from what today's ministries look like. Today, a common ministry is among people and the duties of our ministries typically are associated with helping people. This is a stark contrast from what the priests did.

Throughout the Old Testament, the priests were referred to as "ministers of the Lord." In Chronicles, David says of the priests...

"...for the Lord has chosen them to carry the ark of God and to minister before Him forever." 1 Chronicles 15:2

In fact, there are several verses strewn throughout Deuteronomy and 1 Chronicles that say that the priests were to stand before the Lord and minister; that they were to minister to Him forever. 1 Samuel tells us the same about Samuel as a young boy.

"...the boy ministered to the Lord before Eli the priest."
1 Samuel 2:11

Hannah, his mother who had prayed to receive a son, made the promise that she would give her son up to the Lord (for ministry). Giving Samuel to the Lord meant that he would spend his life in the temple performing the priestly duties of ministering to God through the care of the temple.

Who did the priests spend their days ministering to? The Lord. Their daily operations consisted of ministering to God. That is what they did! This is why they were referred to as ministers of the Lord, NOT of the people.

The priests' only service to the people is what came out of their ministering to God. It was through their continual care of the temple; this was their act of worship. Since the temple was designed to be a dwelling place for God and where the people could meet with God, the care of the temple was very important. The priests functioned as mediators of God's presence and were responsible for the day-to-day operation of the cultic sites, whether it was the tabernacle, local shrines, or the temple in Jerusalem. Their focus was on ministering to God first THROUGH the care of the temple. This was their first work. Furthermore, if the priests had forsaken their first work, the people then would have suffered as a result. This is why it was so important that the priests kept their priorities to ministry before the Lord first!

I would like to throw in that WE are the temple today and we could learn much from the importance of the daily tending to our own temples. This is why "self-ministry" or "self-care" IS biblical and will be discussed further in the chapters to come. But for now, let's see the pattern that God set here through the priesthood; ministry to God first, ministry to the temple, and then out of that, the people received ministry. Do you see it? God-reconciliation, self-reconciliation, then reconciliation with others.

Love God, love self, love others; minister to God, minister to self, minister to others. This takes us right back to the greatest commandment.

JESUS THE HIGH PRIEST

Jesus Himself was the High Priest and His ministry was to God first. It was through His service and ministry to the Father that we now also have access to God. Just like the priests in the Old Testament, Jesus served as a mediator of God's presence, and still does.

"Seeing then that we have a great High Priest who has passed through the heavens, Jesus the Son of God, let us hold fast our confession. For we do not have a High Priest who cannot sympathize with our weaknesses, but was in all points tempted as we are, yet without sin. Let us therefore come boldly to the throne of grace, that we may obtain mercy and find grace to help in time of need." Hebrews 4:14-16

Jesus prepared the way for man by ministering to God first...just like the priests in the Old Testament.

WE AS THE PRIESTHOOD

"...you also, as living stones, are being built up a spiritual house, a holy priesthood, to offer up spiritual sacrifices acceptable to God through Jesus Christ." 1 Peter 2:5

"But you are a chosen generation, a royal priesthood, a holy nation, His own special people that you may proclaim the praises of Him who called you out of darkness into His marvelous light." 1 Peter 2:9

God has called us into the ministry TO HIM. Our "job" is to live a life of sacrifice and proclaim His praises...continuously. We are to "minister before Him forever." (1 Chronicles 15:2.)

I can't help but think of a woman named Anna "who did not depart from the temple, but served God with fastings and prayers night and day." (Luke 2:37) Her non-stop ministry to God is what gave her the eyes to recognize what all the world couldn't see, the Redeemer while He was yet in infant stage. (We could learn a lot from that right there!) Likewise, your ministry should be to God first. He is your first love; He is your first work!

We also serve as a mediator of God's presence. As we stay connected to Him through our ministry to Him, we become the "presence" of heaven on earth for others. I like to remind people that our job is to cause earth to look a little more like heaven. This is our ministry, and it flows out of our ministry to God. As we daily pour out our lives and proclaim His praises, His presence becomes seen in our countenance in everything we do. We should be like Moses whose face shone after his time with the Lord! And, much like the priests in the Old Testament, our own ministry to God will have an effect on the people around us.

MARY OR MARTHA

Though Jesus did indeed come to serve, He was clear that ministry to people should never come before ministry to God. The story of Mary and Martha is a great example.

"Now it happened as they went that He entered a certain village; and a certain woman named Martha welcomed Him into her house. And she had a sister called Mary, who also sat at Jesus' feet and heard His word. But Martha was distracted with much serving, and she approached Him and said, 'Lord, do You not care that my sister has left me to serve alone? Therefore tell her to help me.' And Jesus answered and said to her, 'Martha, Martha, you are worried and troubled about many things. But one thing is needed, and Mary has chosen that good part, which will not be taken away from her.'"
Luke 10:38-42

Jesus uses this opportunity to teach that there is beauty in prioritizing your ministry to God. Mary was found sitting at Jesus' feet listening to His voice; she was totally absorbed in His presence. She was "Seeking FIRST the Kingdom of God" (Matthew 6:33), and her First Love was evident by her demonstration.

Martha, on the other hand, was distracted away from the presence of Jesus. Why? Because of her duties to man. I think we could learn a lot just from that statement. Because of the cultural rules along with religious duties, Martha missed out on sitting at the feet of Christ. GULP! I am feeling a sting of conviction even as I write this.

On another note, notice that Martha not only misses out, but she is angry and bitter about the whole situation. Here she is doing the "right thing" while Mary chooses to set a boundary and say "no" to duty and is reaping peace and joy. Sound familiar? Not setting boundaries or doing what isn't in your heart will often cause anger and bitterness. The point isn't that we shouldn't serve; the point is serving man shouldn't trump serving God.

Instead, our focus daily should be to minister to God, that's it! This is the "one thing that is needed," it is the "good part." The Message says it like this:

"One thing only is essential, and Mary has chosen it–it's the main course, and won't be taken from her."

I think it is sad that we often hear women who are known for serving a lot (whether compelled by God or guilt) called "Marthas." We give them that term as if it is a good thing, but it is not! Too often, our Martha tendencies are rooted in guilt, or the need to be in control, or the need to be needed...I call this the "martyr syndrome," which many of us ladies are very good at. I mean, let's be honest, we love to see the immediate results of helping someone, and we love the way it makes us feel. The problem is that this makes the service more about ourselves and the person we are serving than it is about God. But notice that Jesus says nothing good about Martha's choice in that moment, not one thing. He does however state that He will not rebuke Mary or allow any guilt to come upon her. The results of each lady's choices were vastly different. One had a worried and troubled soul (some versions say worried, bothered, and anxious), while the other was at peace. I am curious, which one do you connect with the most?

Now, don't hear what I am not saying. I am not saying that we shouldn't be servants or minister to people. What I AM saying is that people should not be your first ministry, God should be!

MAKING THE CONNECTION

I am ever-thankful for the words that those two prophets had spoken to me and that I was beginning to realize what they meant. Through this passage, the Lord revealed to me that I had become like Martha, busy with the ministry. All that was urgent distracted me and I was forsaking what was important...the "one thing that was needed," which was for me to minister to God. The results were much like Martha's in that I was filled with much angst. I was troubled frequently because there were so many variables that I could not control and frankly, my health was struggling as well (which I will expound on in the chapters to come). I knew that the Lord was calling me back to my first work, which was to focus on ministering to Him; that I was to seek first His Kingdom (Matthew 6:33), which by the way is a passage that attacks the spirit of worry.

I was ready. I wanted to get back to my ministry to God!

PRAYER PRACTICE

God, what a beautiful Father You are; Your kindness and gentleness cannot be described. I thank You for the way You bring my heart back to Yours. I love that You never let me stray, but that You allure me back into Your arms. I thank You for the wisdom that You have generously given to me through Your Holy Spirit, that I might know how to hear and implement Your word and Your truth in my life. Thank You for hanging on to me and for leading me down the road that is lit by Your light and leads straight to Paradise.

In Jesus' name, Amen.

Chapter 11
The Lampstand

"Remember therefore from where you have fallen; repent and do the first works, or else I will come to you quickly and remove your lampstand from its place." Revelation 2:5

THE LOSS OF THE LAMPSTAND

This part of this passage from Revelation tells us that not turning back to your first works after drifting away will result in a loss. It is the loss of the lampstand.

The lampstand is first mentioned in the book of Exodus. It was to provide light for the tabernacle. And, since it was the only source of light within the tabernacle, it was important that the lampstand was maintained. It required regular attention, which was part of the duty of the priests.

"And you shall command the children of Israel that they bring you pure oil of pressed olives for the light, to cause the lamp to burn continually. In the tabernacle of meeting, outside the veil, which is before the Testimony, Aaron and his sons shall tend it from evening until morning before the Lord. It shall be a statute forever to their generations on behalf of the children of Israel."
Exodus 27:20-21

"Command the children of Israel that they bring to you pure oil of pressed olives for the light, to make the lamps burn continually. Leviticus 24:2

"Aaron shall burn on it sweet incense every morning; when he tends the lamps, he shall burn incense on it." Exodus 30:7

Twice a day, morning and evening, a priest tended to the wick and replenished the pure beaten olive oil inside the lamps. There was no room for distraction or getting sucked up in the cares of the world outside of the tabernacle. To do so would result in the loss of light.

THE LAMPSTAND IN US

The lampstand was a prophetic picture of the light Christ would be for us as His children. Remember, we are the temple of God, and Jesus is our source of light.

"Then Jesus spoke to them again, saying, 'I am the light of the world. He who follows Me shall not walk in darkness, but have the light of life.'" John 8:12

Once you come to know Christ personally, He illuminates things within you that you otherwise would not know. However, like the priests, you must tend to the "lampstand" of Jesus within you.

TENDING TO THE LAMPSTAND

The wick of the lampstand required regular trimming. If the wick of a candle gets too long, it no longer burns from the wax, but rather from the wick itself. It is much the same with an oil lamp, if the wick gets too long, it no longer draws its flame from the oil, but rather burns from the wick. This has two results. First, the flame becomes smoky and dark, which means it does not burn as bright and the flame is not pure. Second, the flame will not last as long. Although it looks bigger and stronger, it is short-lived.

Isn't this true of us as well? Understand that the oil of the lampstand represents the Holy Spirit, and the wick represents our flesh. When we are not burning from the oil of the Holy Spirit, but rather are burning out of our flesh, our flame is dim, smoky and short-lived! This is why it is so important to keep our "flesh" trimmed. When our flesh grows, we will no longer be relying on the Holy Spirit to inflame us for life. Instead, we will be working out of our own strength, knowledge, energy, etc. Keeping the wick trimmed forces the wick to draw its flame from the oil, so it is with us. As we walk in surrender and humility to the Lord, our flesh is diminished and we therefore draw from the Holy Spirit in all things.

This is also why we must keep the oil of the Holy Spirit fresh! This happens as we stir up our intimacy with God DAILY or engage in the love exchange with Him. This means we saturate ourselves in His love and simply respond to that love. It is loving and being loved intentionally by God and with God. We should never think that a weekly soaking in the oil would saturate our wick enough to last throughout the week. The flame will be smoky, impure, and could potentially go out before the next soaking. Just like the oil of the lampstand required daily tending, so does our relationship with God. The more we seek Him and sit at His feet, the more He fills us up with the freshness of His Holy Spirit. It is not about getting more of Him, but rather about engaging with Him and in the love cycle of loving and being loved. This is what stimulates the continual infilling of Him.

"And do not be drunk with wine, in which is dissipation; but be filled with the Spirit." Ephesians 5:18

This phrase in Greek means a *continual filling*, in fact, some versions read: "be being filled." This is what it means to replenish the oil of the lamp. I can't help but think about the parable of the wise and foolish virgins from Matthew 25.

"Then the kingdom of heaven shall be likened to ten virgins who took their lamps and went out to meet the bridegroom. Now five of them were wise, and five were foolish. Those who were foolish took their lamps and took no oil with them, but the wise took oil in their vessels with their lamps. But while the bridegroom was delayed, they all slumbered and slept.

"And at midnight a cry was heard: 'Behold, the bridegroom is coming; go out to meet him!' Then all those virgins arose and trimmed their lamps. And the foolish said to the wise, 'Give us some

of your oil, for our lamps are going out.' But the wise answered, saying, 'No, lest there should not be enough for us and you; but go rather to those who sell, and buy for yourselves. 'And while they went to buy, the bridegroom came, and those who were ready went in with him to the wedding; and the door was shut."
Matthew 25:1-10

Although all ten of the virgins had lamps, and all ten had trimmed their lamps, only five were prepared to replenish their oil. And think about it, a lamp with no oil is no good. It is completely ineffective, even if the wick IS trimmed! Therefore, just keeping our wick trimmed and "nicely groomed" isn't what God is looking for. He is looking for those whose lives burn with the fire of the Holy Ghost! Otherwise, we simply are living religiously.

God has put the lampstand of His presence in you, but if you are not intentional to engage in His presence, then the lampstand will not be illuminated in you and through you. This is the loss that will be experienced when your ministry to God loses first place in your heart. Conversely, you can light that lampstand ablaze by stirring up the love you have for Him through your worship of Him in every moment.

❧PRAYER PRACTICE

God, I thank You for putting the fire of the Holy Ghost inside of me. I bow my knee to You and humble myself before Your presence and receive Your love to the fullest measure. I remember You through the watches of the night and think of You when I lay on my bed. I extol You with my whole heart and my lips proclaim Your praise! Stir it up Lord, pour forth Your holy oil and replenish the stale with the freshness of Your love. May I burn brightly all the days of my life.

In Jesus' name I pray, Amen.

Chapter 12
Reconciled with the Paradise of God

This is what it means to minister to God: to keep my flesh in check and keep the Holy Spirit stirred up, but what does it LOOK like to minister to God? Now that we know that God is telling us that we need to prioritize our ministry to Him first and keep His fire lit, how do we do that? What does it mean to live daily like Mary did in that moment? I wondered that myself when I was overtaken with responsibilities of the ministry that monopolized my time, my thoughts, and my energy. How was I supposed to shift my life without dropping the ball? In His faithfulness, the Lord reminded me of the woman who anointed the feet of Jesus in Luke 7:36-50.

This story is about a sinful woman who enters into a room full of men to sit at the feet of Jesus. Much like Mary, according to the culture and religion, she should have only been entering the room for the purpose of serving the men. However, she was drawn to the presence of love...true love. She isn't forced to worship Him, she isn't coerced or commanded, but rather, she is allured.

I wrote this blog a few years back about this woman in regard to worship, but I think it summarizes my point of ministering to God as well.

The woman who anointed Jesus demonstrated the essence of worship in that she ministered directly to Him. She was unaware of her surroundings, wasn't influenced by those who were staring at her, but rather in an uninhibited passion she solely focused on Jesus, and in His presence all she knew of herself was suddenly shifted.

Her entire identity as Prostitute no longer existed.

Simon comes along and accuses Jesus of not knowing who and what manner of woman this was. Although Jesus knew everything about her, I don't believe for a moment that He saw a prostitute. That was not her identity to Him. Instead He saw the real her and who she was created to be; He saw her design.

What a tipping point this was for this woman, to sit at the feet of Jesus and in that one moment become completely transformed and set free from the lie that she had been living.

And so it is with us, as we live in worship of Him, ministering to Jesus first, sitting at His feet, pouring out our praise and our adoration, not worrying about everybody around us:

- *being uninhibited*
- *being willing to focus in on just Him and Him alone*
- *weeping in His presence*
- *sacrificing our hair and our body to minister to Him*

For we, as His holy priests, have the honor of stepping into the Most Holy Place and serving at His altar first. For it is in that place that we are changed. We no longer see ourselves as the world sees us. We no longer see ourselves through our own eyes or even through the mistakes or the failures of our life. But rather we see ourselves in the eyes of God.

Consider what the woman saw when she gazed into the eyes of Jesus.

I know she saw love, a love she had never seen and never experienced before, for it was not a love of this world. But she saw the love of an almighty God. Consider how she felt when she walked into that room. And then consider how she felt when she walked out. There was a spiritual transformation in just one moment, everything was shifted, a tipping point.

And so I step in to minister to my God every day, going in as one person but coming out as another.

I know that every moment at His feet is shifting things in the spirit realm for me, transforming me, making me more into His likeness. For I go in as myself, but I come out more like Him. Oh that we would get this and understand just how much takes place in our ministry to Him; things unseen, yet more real than the things we do see. It's not something that can be explained or reasoned because it is supernatural.

Do you see how this is a picture of ministry to God? It is intentionally worshipping Him daily. It is stopping what you are doing and setting aside the world to enter into the Most High Place. There are so many things and people that become our objects of worship that we tend to lose the simplicity of God being God. Urgencies and *"have-tos"* crowd Him out and eventually our fire gets dimmer and dimmer, and our passion gets less and less.

This woman demonstrated her ministry to God by offering up a sacrifice and pouring out her praises upon the feet of Jesus... literally. Remember the verses in 1 Peter 2 from the previous chapter?

"...you also, as living stones, are being built up a spiritual house, a holy priesthood, to offer up spiritual sacrifices acceptable to God through Jesus Christ." 1 Peter 2:5

"But you are a chosen generation, a royal priesthood, a holy nation, His own special people that you may proclaim the praises of Him who called you out of darkness into His marvelous light." 1 Peter 2:9

I can't help but think of how the Bible describes golden bowls full of incense "which are the prayers of the saints" (Revelation 5:8). In other words, the prayers and praises of God's people collectively fill heavenly bowls with sweet aroma, much like the burnt offerings did in days of the Old Testament. This is yet another picture that God laid out for us in regard to cultivating His Presence. Our proclamations of praise rise up to the nostrils of God...weird thought, I know, but accurate! When we praise God, it is to heaven like when we burn bowls of incense in our house and a sweet aroma is released throughout each room. God loves the scent of our praises and is honored by them.

BEING RECONCILED THROUGH OUR MINISTRY

I love the simplicity of worshipping God. It is easy and freeing! I don't have to think about all the cares of the world; I get to be still and be loved. I don't have to put on a mask or worry about what He will think; I get to be transparent and honest. I don't have to keep up a wall or protect myself; I get to be vulnerable and connect on a deeper level. I get to love and to be loved just the way I am and the best I know how in that moment. There is no judgment at His feet, only love and acceptance.

This act of ministry is the "one thing that is needed" that Jesus was speaking of in Luke 10 about Mary. It is the "good part" because this is where things get reconciled.

It is where the places in my heart and mind that are out of alignment are made congruent with His. They are reconciled; brought back together with God. I find a great exchange at the feet of Jesus. Through my worship, I am drawn to pour out my own perceptions, thoughts, opinions, feelings, etc. and choose His. It is a Divine exchange compelled by the stirring of the Holy Spirit as love is being exchanged. It is like when the water that was turned into wine inside a vessel in John 2. Nobody knows how it happened, or when it happened, but in the end, there was evidence of a supernatural occurrence. This is the process that God does inside of us to reconcile our REAL identity, which is our God identity, His design for us.

I believe David was very practiced at ministering to the Lord. We see evidence of that throughout the Psalms, which are basically just records of his praises and worship to God. He knew that ministering to God was the "one thing that was needed." It was necessary!

> "One thing I have desired of the Lord,
> That will I seek:
> That I may dwell in the house of the Lord
> All the days of my life,
> To behold the beauty of the Lord,
> And to inquire in His temple.
> For in the time of trouble

He shall hide me in His pavilion;
In the secret place of His tabernacle
He shall hide me;
He shall set me high upon a rock." Psalm 27:4-5

This is one of many examples that David demonstrates for us throughout the Psalms. No wonder God referred to him as "a man after God's own heart." However, we must choose to engage in this. God is not going to force us or command us to worship Him. He is a loving God who invites us to enter into His Presence. We should be drawn by His love, much like Mary and the woman who anointed the feet of Jesus were. God has lain out before us the opportunity to come into the fullness of life through His spirit, but we have to respond actively. We must be doers of the Word and not hearers only (see James 1). As we do, we will overcome and the fruit of life will be released!

THE FRUIT OF HIS PARADISE

"He who has an ear let him hear what the Spirit says to the churches. To him who overcomes I will give to eat from the tree of life, which is in the midst of the Paradise of God." Revelation 2:7

Where do we find the fruit of the tree of life? In the midst of the Paradise of God. And what do we find in the midst of His paradise? The fruit of life! Do you see the cycle? When we engage in ministry to God, we step into His Paradise and find the fruit that He has made available to us, and the more we taste and see that the Lord is good (Psalm 34), the more we live in the Paradise of God; it becomes our normal. We must realize that we are spirit beings that have human experiences. There should be no such thing as having spiritual moments; our entire life should be a spiritual experience. This is what it means to reside in the Paradise of God and eat continually from His tree of life. And this is what God desired for us all along.

"And out of the ground the Lord God made every tree grow that is pleasant to the sight and good for food. The tree of life was also in the midst of the garden..." Genesis 2:9

Think with me for a moment about what it must have been like for Adam and Eve to dwell in the Garden of Eden. They walked with God daily and conversed freely with Him. His presence was continually with them; that was their normal. And, not only that, they were naked, which signifies that there was no shame or need to be covered. They felt free to be completely seen, transparent, and vulnerable. They knew that they were loved, and their lives simply consisted of loving Him back. They lived the love cycle with God...to love and to be loved is all they knew and their lives were an expression of that truth.

Well, we know how the story goes and how the enemy deceived and manipulated Eve by getting her to doubt what she knew to be true. Thus, sin entered into the world and Adam and Eve experienced the separation that came because of sin. Ever since that moment, God has continued to love us as His children and went as far as sacrificing His one and only Son to reconcile that separation. That reconciliation includes bringing us back into the Paradise of God. It is not just so that we can go to heaven someday, but so we can live like Adam and Eve in the Garden of Eden.

Through our ministry to God, we are reconciled with what is true—that in His presence, we are loved. Like Mary and the woman who anointed the feet of Jesus, there is freedom and ease in that place; the place where all fears and the pressures of the world dissipate. Only His love is perfect enough to cast that out! (1 John 4:18) As we come to Him to proclaim His praises and pour out our hearts, we will experience this truth more and more.

"Come to Me, all you who labor and are heavy laden, and I will give you rest. Take My yoke upon you and learn from Me, for I am gentle and lowly in heart, and you will find rest for your souls. For My yoke is easy and My burden is light." Matthew 11:28-30

There is ease when you are yoked to God and learn how to let Him love you. This is where you will find rest for your soul.

This is also the first step to establishing healthy relationships because if you don't know the love of God, you don't really know love at all. It is through abiding in His love that you learn what love is.

"And we have known and believed the love that God has for us. God is love, and he who abides in love abides in God, and God in him."
1 John 4:16

Reconciliation starts when you are reconciled with God through Christ. But as we have learned through these past chapters, we must understand the part we play in walking in that reconciliation in order to be restored into His paradise and reap the fruit. So start with practicing the love cycle with God. Connect with Him freely and go before Him completely naked and show Him everything that is in your heart...the good, the bad and the ugly. He already knows it's there, He is just waiting for you to expose it to Him. The invitation will always stand, His love for you is not in question, the only question is: Will you allow yourself to be loved and love in response?

PRAYER PRACTICE

God, thank You for teaching me how to be loved. I thank You for the freedom that I have to connect with You just as I am. I find no judgment in Your presence, but You accept me, all of me, and You love everything about me. Thank You that You are enamored by me! I stand before You and take off all my masks and expose all of who I am to You. It is Your perfect love that has cast out all my fear and freed me to love and to be loved.

In Jesus' name I pray, Amen.

Part 2
Self

Chapter 13
Falling in Love with You

We have spent the last few chapters learning what it means to "love the Lord your God with all your heart, with all your soul, and with all your strength," and the importance of making God our "first love" by ministering to Him and cultivating intimacy through intentional connection with the Holy Spirit. This absolutely must remain at the core of establishing healthy relationships because it is only in His presence that you will come to see your design as He sees it. But there is a next step that is often missed in reconciliation, and that is reconciling and getting connected with yourself. Having a healthy, intimate relationship with God is one thing, and having a healthy relationship with yourself is another. In these next few chapters you will learn the importance of the love cycle within you, and what it means to minister to yourself. You must fall in love with your "God design."

A HEALTHY VIEW OF SELF

"You shall love the Lord your God with all your heart, with all your soul, with all our strength, and with all your mind, and your neighbor as yourself." Luke 10:27

Looking at the greatest commandment, I think we too often miss the part that says to love you, meaning you love who you are and have a healthy view of yourself. Don't look at the order that this verse is written, but rather look at the heart of what is written. God stresses that to the same degree to which I am able to love myself will I love another person. Note that He is not commanding that we love ourselves, but rather He knows that our self-love is a natural standard or natural measurement by which we will pour out love on someone else. It is a frame of reference. He does something similar in Luke 6:31: "Do to others as you would have them do to you." He is able to use your self-respect as a standard to which you measure how to respect someone else. In other words, your love and respect for others is directly proportionate to the way you love and respect yourself.

Typically the WAY I love myself is the same way I will love someone else. For example, if I love myself critically and struggle with self-condemnation, then I might likely "love" others with a critical spirit and communicate condemnation towards them, even if I don't intend to. If I struggle with insecurities and fears then I will be less likely to love others freely and vulnerably. It may cause me to love them enviously or to feel inferior. I may also respond quickly in anger or defense when I feel "threatened" because of my own insecurities. I also might hide my true thoughts or emotions for fear of being rejected. In all of this, lack of self-reconciliation with who God has designed you to be will affect your relationships with others. Self-love plays a huge part in how you love others, meaning how you express love will be influenced by the way you first love yourself.

We have already discovered that we learn who we are through our ministry to God and that falling in love with God is imperative. Well, I would like to propose that it is time that we fall in love with ourselves and the beauty of who He has created each of us to be. I mean, if the Father finds us worthy of lavishing His love upon you, then shouldn't you also relish in who you are and be OK with lavishly loving yourself? Perhaps we should show more respect for our God design and actively engage in self-ministry. And I am talking body, soul and spirit by the way...loving our full self.

"For we are His workmanship, created in Christ Jesus for good works, which God prepared beforehand that we should walk in them." Ephesians 2:10

The word *workmanship* here comes from the Greek word *poiema* which is the derivative of the word "poem." O man, I love this! Call me sappy, but I have a soft spot in my heart for poetry. I find poems to be both passionate and often very romantic. They typically reflect the depths of someone's heart; their secret place released into words! The creative writings are the outpouring of all that is within the heart and mind of someone as they speak a message or story they long to tell. Likewise, we are God's "poiema," written to reflect the depths of His heart and created to speak His message and live His purpose. We are the outpouring of His heart; His secret place manifest through His prized creations; you and I. This is what we are falling in love with...ourselves as the workmanship of God...created by His hand and poured of the depths of his heart.

Before I can walk in healthy relationships with others, I must be in love with who God has designed me to be and the plan He has for my life. However, this concept seems to be so challenging, even to mature believers. I fear that we have lost a love for self, we no longer teach the importance of it. This has left us victims to the pressures of others, the pressures of the world, and our own self-pressures...trying to measure up, fit in and be loved out of fear and desperation. This does not make for healthy connections.

PRAYER PRACTICE

God, I am in love with the story You are telling through my life. I embrace every day like a line spoken in a poem...each one with purpose and intent. What a beautiful picture You have painted through my life. I love the colors of every day and the design that is coming forth. You are the Master Artist and there is no flaw in my design!

In Jesus' name I pray, Amen.

THE ART OF BEING YOURSELF

I recently watch a Ted Talk called "The Art of Being Yourself" and the speaker talked about how all of life is basically all about discovering who we really are. Whether a believer or not, we often find ourselves asking, "Who am I?" The speaker mentioned that we live life battling between who people say we are, perception; who we want to be, the "wishbone"; and who we really are, the ego. Now, let me sidetrack here for a minute to note that we often give the word "ego" a bad rap. We tend to connect it with having pride, saying things like, "She has an ego" and assume that to mean, "She is arrogant." But ego simply is how someone views himself or herself. It literally means "a sense of personal identity." That being said, we all struggle with waffling back and forth between man's perception, our "wishbone," and our ego. All three of these are a form of perception, which means "the ability to see, hear or become aware of something through the senses."

Let me connect this spiritually. The first one is when you become aware of who you are through the senses of others. The second is when you become aware of who you are through your own senses (your opinions, thoughts, and desires, etc.). And the third is when you become aware of who you are based on God's "senses," which is your REAL personal identity, or your ego. Although we know perceptions don't necessarily reflect facts, whatever perception you agree with will become your personal truth.

The take-away of the message in this Ted Talk was that though we will never live a perception-less life, we could live perception-free, meaning free from influence of the world's perceptions. I agree…the world is full of many perceptions and opinions and too often we allow ourselves to be tossed back and forth by the whims of those perceptions.

So how do we enter into "perception-free" living in a "perception-filled" world? How do we conquer "The Art of Being Yourself?" By settling on God's perception. By seeing, hearing, and becoming aware of who we are through God, which then becomes our personal truth (our ego). I don't have to allow the perceptions of anything, other than God, define me. You see, because I am a spirit-being, although I live in the world, I am not OF the world. Therefore, the world does not define me and I GET to live in it perception-free!

I find it worth noting that the speaker of that Ted Talk also mentioned that a perception-free life means living freed from comparison. How true is that? Because there is nothing that compares with God's perception, which is Truth! The world is filled with all kinds of perceptions and opinions, which can keep us trapped in trying to "live up to" or stuck in continual comparison. However, when you come to realize that God's view is the only one that matters, all other perceptions lose their influence; they no longer have control over you. You must remember that includes your own perception as well. Often, the way we view ourselves is the harshest perception yet. I heard it once said that to be free from you is to find real freedom. This happens as we fall in love with who we are in Christ. Only then, will I be OK with being transparent and vulnerable, thus able to connect and love others, AS I LOVE MYSELF...freely and liberally!

PRAYER PRACTICE

God, open my eyes that I would see myself the way You see me...and then open my heart that I would feel the same way about me as You feel about me. Bring me into alignment with You! I ask that any gap between who You are and who I am be filled so that I am completely hidden in Your Truth. Narrow those places, Lord, and drag my soul in line with Your spirit. Poke me and prod me to respond. Convince me, Lord, of Your Truth about who I am and the beauty I have. I pray that I would come into the fullness of reconciliation that was established on the cross. I shift myself toward Your heart and receive from Your hand all that is right and true!

In Jesus' name I pray, Amen.

Chapter 14
The Many Views of Self-Love

We have already discovered that we learn who we are through our ministry to God. Falling in love with God is imperative and His view is the only one that matters. Talking about this conceptually seems so easy, and it is, but it is also *not* easy because we live in a world that is constantly speaking all kinds of messages that claim to be the truth. This is a part of that "system" I talked about in the first section of this book that influences in ways we aren't even aware throughout our entire life. If we are not careful to KNOW what God says, we will get sucked into false truths and will be molded by the system instead of by God.

This system also has an opinion about self-reconciliation and self-love that is counterintuitive to what the Bible says. There are four major views placed before us in life: the world's view, a religious view, God's view, and then our own view. Let's take a look at the story of the woman who was about to be stoned in John 8 to gain a perspective of the system she lived in and all the opinions it offered.

"Now early in the morning He came again into the temple, and all the people came to Him; and He sat down and taught them. Then the scribes and Pharisees brought to Him a woman caught in adultery. And when they had set her in the midst, they said to Him, 'Teacher, this woman was caught in adultery, in the very act. Now Moses, in the law, commanded us that such should be stoned. But what do You say?' This they said, testing Him, that they might have something of which to accuse Him. But Jesus stooped down and wrote on the ground with His finger, as though He did not hear. So when they continued asking Him, He raised Himself up and said to them, 'He who is without sin among you, let him throw a stone at

her first.' And again He stooped down and wrote on the ground. Then those who heard it, being convicted by their conscience, went out one by one, beginning with the oldest even to the last. And Jesus was left alone, and the woman standing in the midst. When Jesus had raised Himself up and saw no one but the woman, He said to her, 'Woman, where are those accusers of yours? Has no one condemned you?' She said, 'No one, Lord.' And Jesus said to her, 'Neither do I condemn you; go and sin no more.'"
John 8:2-11

There are many lessons that we can learn from this passage, but for the sake of making my point let me simply point out all the perspectives; each one coming with its own perceptions and opinions. First, there is the religious view that is seen through the scribes and the Pharisees. Second, there is the world's view that is seen through the onlookers or those who stood around watching the scene. Third, there is God's view or a biblical view that is seen through Jesus. The last view is the one we often miss...and that is the self-view seen through the woman. This is the system seen in this story and each view has an opinion about the idea of loving yourself.

WORLD-VIEW

The world has a view of self-love that is rooted in pride, with the focus on self-abilities. The biggest contrast to having a biblical view is that of glorifying self instead of glorifying God. Meaning it is all about how your gifts, talents, abilities, looks, job, etc. bring attention to you and establish your value. Although a world-view will tell you that you don't need the accolade of man, the reality is it keeps you stuck in the world's standards and the measures of man. Therefore it thrives off the world's accolades to affirm identity and establish worth.

Because the world has a standard that we have to fit in to, in every situation, we end up struggling with two options: inferiority or superiority. This keeps us stuck in a world of comparison with the world providing our plumb line instead of God. It keeps us looking side to side and we end up either feeling constantly underneath or on top, depending on the standard around us. To combat the threat of inferiority, the world will tell us to boast about our accomplishment and take pride in who we are with the motive to be glorified. It will tell us that to be on top, or superior, we need to measure up to its standards. This is a vicious view that keeps us battling to keep up with what is considered valuable. And because the world's standards are always changing, we have to stay on our toes if we want to be highly valued. From what degree you have, to what style of clothes you wear, to whom you know; the world has a perception. The world bears a classic survival of the fittest mentality, where I don't need to be the BEST me I was created to be, I just need to be better than those around me! "If I can just be superior, then I will be highly esteemed."

This is a big contrast to what God says. God's viewpoint is clear in that in Him we are the head and not the tail, above only and never beneath (see Deuteronomy 28:13). It doesn't matter who you are with or the status of those around you, in God's economy, you ARE positioned superiorly. In God's economy, no one compares to you!

Comparison is a challenge that we run into in the housing program. We see the ladies allowing the performance (or lack of performance) navigate what they do or do not accomplish. We have to continually remind them that their own plan, established with God and encouraged by us, is what should compel them. This is why farmers and trainers often use yokes with blinders on their animals. A horse running a race should not allow the horses around them to set their pace, rather they should run according to their OWN ability under the navigation of their rider. Furthermore, they should only run the race that has been set for them.

"Let us lay aside every weight, and the sin which so easily ensnares us, and let us run with endurance the race that is set before us, looking unto Jesus, the author and finisher of our faith."
Hebrews 12:1-2

The world-view is a snare that will keep you running;

hopping from path to path trying to figure out who you really are and how to measure up and find your sense of worth. It is relentless and will exhaust you. You run and will never find rest. It will tell you to boast in yourself and use your gifts and talents to get to where you want to be.

To borrow Whitney Houston's words, the world will tell you that "learning to love yourself is the greatest love of all" and while I agree that we need to learn to love ourselves, the question is for what purpose? Why? If it is to simply glorify you and to be the best in the room then your motive is navigated by a world-view.

RELIGIOUS VIEW

The religious view is almost opposite of the world-view in that it is all about lowering yourself and making yourself the most humble in the room. I think in attempt to counteract the world-view of loving self, the religious view presents a self-abasing mentality. There is a cautious approach to self-love, so as not to err on the side of pride. There is a thin line between the words "humility" and "humiliating." And somewhere I fear that in our attempt to walk in humility, we end up humiliating our God-design and the tenacity and boldness that comes with it.

When David showed up to the battleline offering to fight Goliath, he was accused of being arrogant. It was said that he had pride in his heart (1 Samuel 17) by his own brothers (God's army). Why? Because he was confident in who he was and the right God had given them to that land? Does that make him prideful, or does it make him bold and confident? David was sure of the design God had in mind for the Israelites, and he was bold, knowing that in God, he was the head and not the tail! We must not interpret tenacity of the spirit as pride of the heart. One is a God-view of self-love, while the other is a religious view. We see the same boldness in David in 2 Samuel 6 when he danced before the Lord, unashamed and without fear...in his underwear! And a religious view rose up against such freedom and confidence. His own wife acted as if his actions were humiliating, when in reality, for a king to take off his robe and dance so freely was probably one of the most humble acts we see in Scripture.

I had a similar experience when I was called to travel and speak in my ministry. When I found the courage to communicate that I felt an anointing on my life, I was discouraged by many of my brothers and sisters in Christ. It was almost as if they were shocked or disgraced that I would speak about my own gifts and calling so confidently. I was even intentional to clarify that I knew this was God's calling and God's gifts. I was often dismissed and placated with phrases like, "Well, if you *think* it is God's will..." or "Well, if you think you need a website for God to promote you..." I was also "warned" over and over that I needed to stay "humble" if I wanted God to use me. Now, forgive me, but I personally think that statement is rooted in works and pride and dismisses the grace of God. Here is the fact; without Christ there are none of us who are good enough, humble enough, or righteous enough to carry God's anointing or to do His work. It is all Him! His grace favors us with His gifts and by His grace we are imbued with His power through the Holy Spirit. Now, I don't know about you, but I think that is worthy of boasting about! That is exactly my point. God's presence lives in each of us and He works through us...He is always doing something, and what He does is ALWAYS good. Therefore, boasting about what He is doing through my life is simply acknowledging that He is at work. Furthermore, NOT to boast about the work that comes forth is to insinuate that God is doing nothing through my life. I will not agree with that. A religious view will tell you that it is haughty to boast in your gifts and to love who God has created you to be. But God's view of self-love says that to love ourselves is to honor God and His workmanship in us!

I am bothered by the fact that it is often considered haughty to even accept a compliment for what God is doing, and as believers we have become uncomfortable receiving them. I have learned to confidently rejoice when someone acknowledges my efforts to partner with God and practice His gifts. There is nothing wrong with standing amazed by how God is working in you and through you. Furthermore, we should make it a habit to acknowledge God for the ways He is using us. It is healthy and God-honoring to say, "God is using me to accomplish some incredible work" or "I am blessed to see His love pouring out of my life" or "I am praising God for the way He used me today." This is simply agreeing with God that I am valuable in the kingdom and my design is effective. This is God's view of self-love.

GUARDING YOUR DESIGN

God wants us to love our design to the point of guarding it, which means saying no sometimes and putting our design and us first. I know what you are thinking...how do we reconcile passages like Philippians 2 that instruct:

"Let nothing be done through selfish ambition or conceit, but in lowliness of mind, let each esteem others better than himself. Let each of us look not only for his own interests, but also for the interests of others." Verses 2-3

I have had people use this passage to justify why someone in their life should lay aside their own needs to the point of unhealthy boundaries...or no boundaries at all. We cannot pull verses away from the heart of God; we must see them in the context of His love. First of all, this passage DOES say to look out for your own interests, which I think we often miss and don't quote! In our desire to put the interests of others first, we should not dismiss our own. Secondly, these verses are more about addressing the heart than the action. To prioritize self out of selfishness or conceit is to function according to the world-view...in arrogance and comparison. However, to NOT prioritize yourself at all because you've been told it's selfish is to function out of a religious view and sense of duty. Neither is God's view of loving self.

When my kids were little and played with others, if they were fighting over what to do, I would often quote this passage, exhorting my kids to put the interest of their friends first. However, as teenagers, this was NOT my advice. Instead, I encouraged them to stick with what they knew to be right in their own minds and to guard their hearts by putting their future first. I was in a sense saying, "Prioritize your own interests." Think about it, if your child had a friend who wanted them to go drinking, you would not counsel them to put their friend's interest first. Instead you would tell them to prioritize their own interest. It is never a good idea to counsel someone to put first what could potentially steal his or her future, purpose, design, or sanity. And frankly, a good friend wouldn't ask you to!

Our residents have a habit of prioritizing everything and everyone else before themselves. We have to continually remind them that they are in a season in which they *should* be selfish about their own lives for the purpose of healing. But because they have lived in search of love and acceptance, in their desperation to be "liked" in the home, they often sacrifice what is best for them and their children to "help" another resident. They lack in setting healthy boundaries and I cannot tell you how many times a woman has not made her own goals because she became wrapped up in someone else's life, abandoning her own hula-hoop and forfeiting her forward movement. At the core of this is the inability to recognize the value of one's own life and her design. Their fear of rejection is rooted in not being reconciled with God's perfect love and she simply doesn't know the value of her God-design.

We must not pull the Philippians 2 verses away from God's heart. When we do, we distort the spirit of the law, making it the letter of the law, which is a religious view. We must understand the love that God has for us as the basis for every scripture. It is His heart to teach us how to guard His design.

Those with a religious view of self-love will say their motive is to prevent pride and self-glorification. In their attempt to keep that at bay, the religious view damages the beauty of being in love with who God has created you to be. You must understand the importance of your God-design and be willing to be tenacious for it.

SELF-VIEW

Your own view of self-love is highly influenced by many factors around you that will ultimately affect how you love yourself. One's understanding of self-love tends to swing to either viewing self too innocently (pride) or too harshly (guilt and condemnation). We come under the influence of the world-view or religious view because it is the message that is all around us. This is why it is so difficult to simply see ourselves through God's eyes.

"But with me it is a very small thing that I should be judged by you or by a human court. In fact, I do not even judge myself. For I know of nothing against myself, yet I am not justified by this; but He who judges me is the Lord." 1 Corinthians 4:3

It is our tendency to allow everything BUT God judge who we are and the choices that we make. Think with me for a moment about the story of the Good Samaritan. This story is told by Jesus as an example of what it looks like to love your neighbor. But I want to point out a concept that I think we miss. Most often it is assumed that the Priest and the Levite passed by the man in need because of selfishness or fear. I think we miss out on the root issue. I believe the cause of their selfishness or fear was rooted in the lack of their own reconciliation with God's love. Their identities were rooted in their culture and religion and not in God. In other words, they were navigated by their systems. Jesus used this story to shatter that mindset. Seeing ourselves through the eyes of our culture will squelch our self-love and therefore the freedom we have to love our neighbors.

I recently spoke at a Ladies Conference titled "Legacy." Included in my teaching were the ways we often let our heritage, in other words our genetic make-up and past experiences, define us. This is all a part of that system I keep referring to. Our heritage is not what defines our legacy because our legacy is rooted in our God-design, not in our genetics or anything in our past. Our love for self must be lined up or reconciled with God's love for us, period! Anything else will diminish the love that He wants you to have for yourself.

GOD'S VIEW

I have tried to include how God's view of self-love is different from the world's system throughout this chapter. Your system ultimately will influence your concept of loving yourself. God wants you to love who you are. His view of self-love is rooted in creation. It has always been His intention for you to walk passionately in your God-purpose. He knows your design and He reveals it to you as you pursue loving and being loved by Him. Being rooted in Him is so valuable; it confirms who you are and the beauty of your design and silences every other voice. There is no view like God's view...and He desires for you to fall in love with what He has put in you and what He has planned for you. In this you can be confident! Your confidence should not be in your education nor your credentials; not in the world's opinion nor in your job. It should definitely not be in your relationships nor in your heritage. Your confidence must be in who God has created you to be. Listening to other opinions will cheat you of your fullness in Christ and the true beauty of loving yourself and your design.

"As you therefore have received Christ Jesus the Lord, so walk in Him, rooted and built up in Him and established in the faith, as you have been taught, abounding in it with thanksgiving. Beware lest anyone cheat you through philosophy and empty deceit, according to the tradition of men, according to the basic principles of the world, and not according to Christ. For in Him dwells all the fullness of the Godhead bodily; and you are complete in Him, who is the head of all principality and power." Colossians 2:6-10

The basic principles of the world is your system. I think it is worthy to note that many versions say not to be "taken captive" by the principles of the world instead of using the word "cheated." Either way, it is fair to say that the world's system will cheat you of the freedom you have in Christ. Not just freedom FROM, but freedom TO. We get to love who we are because God does; and HE is the head of ALL principality and power. This means His Truth is the final Truth!

God is not the author of self-condemnation or guilt. He does not author self-critical thinking nor words that speak less of who we are. He is the author of exhortation and He encourages and speaks life into dead places. He does not search for sin nor does He dwell on the negative. He relishes in the purpose of each person and considers them highly valuable. Any thought less is not of God! We often practice this with others, but we lack in practicing it with ourselves. We must understand that God has Divine purposes and He creates people around those purposes. He is in love with you because He knows your purpose and your design. This is the biblical view of self-love and it is the only view that should matter.

HOW A SKEWED VIEW AFFECTS RELATIONSHIPS

So what does any of this have to do with establishing healthy relationships? Well, because loving yourself is the key to loving others, our concept of self-love will impact our relationships.

A world-view of self-love will tell you that you have the right to be loved and that you should do what ever it takes to make that happen. This thinking is used to justify manipulation or gaslighting techniques in the world's eyes. It will tell you that every relationship is all about you and your happiness and whether or not you are getting everything you want; that you *deserve* love and happiness. The focus is on self and getting your own needs met even if that means being a bulldozer and forcing things at the expense of someone else's needs or desires.

On the other hand, a religious view of self-love will tell you that you should lay down your right to be loved and that you should sacrifice for others to the point of losing your own identity. It will tell you to always put the interests of others first, to the point of unhealthy boundaries. In fact, religion will puff up those who sacrifice to the point of losing their life; the problem is they are not sacrificing FOR Christ; they are sacrificing for others in the name of Christ. I have seen very abusive relationships come out of the religious view because it does not teach or enforce the importance of healthy boundaries. The line between submitting ourselves to one another; laying down our lives in the soul gets distorted into forfeiting our identities and design. We are called to submit, not to be a doormat.

I was not raised according to biblical principles and

therefore learned about self-love from a world's perspective. From my education to my family structure, it was communicated throughout my life that you should pursue your own dreams at all costs, even at the expense of people. I believed that life was like a bucket of crabs and others could be used to climb to the top, and if you saw another crab at the top before you, you pulled them down if they threatened your own success. I learned that no one should get in your way, and that all you needed to succeed was yourself and your own hard work. This meant operating manipulatively when it was necessary, though I did not realize it at the time.

At the age of eighteen, I came to know the Lord Jesus as my Savior and quickly was indoctrinated into a totally different teaching that was the polar opposite to how I was raised. I was taught to rely upon prayer when it came to relationships, that I could communicate my feelings, opinions, desires, and thoughts to a degree, but ultimately I just need to sacrifice all those things, and put the interests of others first. The importance of considering my own heart and mind was taught. In my marriage as well as many other relationships, I began to submit and surrender my heart and mind to such a degree that I was easily manipulated and found myself operating in fear. I felt I had no rights within relationships and was taught that as a Christian, I deserved nothing. There was no discerning between what we deserve and how we are designed. This resulted in my swinging from being overly confident in myself, and my own heart and mind, to having no confidence and ultimately a total loss of my passion and dreams.

I have had to learn to walk in healthy relationships by understanding God's view of self-love. I pray that you are able to see areas in your life where you have been influenced by the many views within your system and how they have potentially kept you from a healthy view of self-love. It is my desire that you gain God's view and begin to practice a self-love that lines up with His heart and your design.

PRAYER PRACTICE

God there are so many opinions in the world that influence the way I love myself and fear of what people will think often sets in. I know that too often I have been accused of being too confident, and other times of being too passive about the gifts and calling You have given me. Listening to all those opinions will drive me nearly crazy. I want to line myself up with You. Show me, Lord, how to love myself in a way that will glorify You. Show me when to put others first, and then show me when to prioritize health and myself. Show me what is best for me. I want to be the best me I can be...for You! This is not about living a better life for me, it is about living the best life for You. I thank You, Lord, that You have taught me how to love myself enough to set boundaries so as not to compromise my design. Thank You for teaching me that You view self-love as good and honoring to Your workmanship. May I continue to guard my heart above all else, for it IS the wellspring of life.

In Jesus' name I pray, Amen.

Chapter 15
Reconciling with You

Though the process of self-reconciliation is not talked about nor taught nearly enough, it is a crucial piece in your walk toward total freedom. In all my years of counseling, I am amazed at how many people come in because of unhealthy relationships. There is nothing that will make someone more miserable than broken relationships that are not reconciled and continue to be points of pressure in a person's life. However, with the majority of those clients, we end up finding the root of their issue actually lies within their own relationship either with God or with themselves; usually both.

RECONCILIATION BRINGS REVELATION

It is uncanny how working to reconcile with God first and self second then lends itself to healing in relationships all around. There is power in self-reconciliation and the revelation it brings to relationships. Reconciliation clears a path and the fog of emotions and thoughts that keep you from seeing things through God's perspective is cleared up as things are brought into alignment with God. Things that suddenly seemed so dramatic are calmed by inner peace; wounds are soothed by His balm, and unhealthy boundaries are no longer tolerated. Self-reconciliation brings revelation, the truth, which then begins to swallow up emotions and thoughts that would keep you stuck. It illuminates and shines light on what is really going on and the spiritual truths behind every situation and every relationship, including your relationship with you. This is why it is so important, without it, you will be enslaved to pretending to be at peace when internally you are tattered and conflicted.

THE HOLDING PATTERN

As a counselor, I have noticed in my own life, and also in the lives of others, that the Lord will often keep us in a holding pattern while we work on things within ourselves. He will allow a season of healing so that we might reconcile things in our own lives. I think it is important to note that He is content to let us stay there as long as necessary. I often say that if God is not changing your circumstances, He is likely changing you. God is more concerned with the status of your heart than the status of your circumstances. In fact, He will use trials and tribulations to refine us and perfect us in Christ.

"My brethren, count it all joy when you fall into various trials, knowing that the testing of your faith produces patience. But let patience have its perfect work, that you may be perfect and complete, lacking nothing." James 1:2-4

God is unwilling for us to be incomplete. He desires for ALL things to be reconciled with Him. This is pleasing to Him.

"For it pleased the Father that in Him all the fullness should dwell, and by Him to reconcile all things to Himself, by Him, whether things on earth or things in heaven, having made peace through the blood of His cross. And you, who once were alienated and enemies in your mind by wicked works, yet now He has reconciled"
Colossians 1:19-22

Though our reconciliation was established at the cross through Jesus, there are areas that have not appropriated the fullness of that reconciliation...places in my mind where I am still at odds with what God says about who I am. The Holy Spirit within me will war with my flesh, which often causes a tossing back and forth within my own heart and mind. In this, I am not experiencing the peace granted me through the blood of Jesus. When I feel this internal conflict, I will often say, "I just need to get this reconciled within me." It is not about reconciling things outside of me or with the people around me, but rather reconciling things in my own heart and mind. I believe this is what the Lord is talking about in Isaiah.

"Come now, and let us reason together." Isaiah 1:18

The Voice says it like this...

"Come on now, let's walk and talk; let's work this out."

In Hebrew, the phrase, "let us reason together" denotes the idea of proving, deciding, or judging. It also includes the idea of being convinced. Reconciliation brings us to a state of being convinced and not conflicted; all things are harmonious and congruous once we decide to settle on what God says. However, getting to that place often requires a season of working things out, or reasoning, with God. This can feel long and dry and isn't always easy, especially when it involves working through hurts or wounds. But you must remember and BE CONFIDENT that God is good and His motive is to completely reconcile you to Him. His desire is to finish what HE started!

"...being confident of this very thing, that He who has begun a good work in you will complete it until the day of Jesus Christ." Philippians 1:6

God wants you to see yourself the way He sees you. He wants you to agree with Him about who you are. It is one thing to say that I believe God thinks I am beautiful, but is another to look in the mirror and say, "I agree, YOU are beautiful." Or to have the knowledge that God loves me, but then to look in the mirror and say, "I agree, YOU are loveable and I love you." This is the challenge that must be overcome if we are going to love and to be loved with the way God has designed us to.

THE WOMAN ABOUT TO BE STONED
Let's go back to the story in John 8 about the woman who was about to be stoned. We talked about the differing perspectives

in that scene, each one having an opinion about how worthy of love she was. I often wonder what was going on in the woman's mind as she looked in the eyes of TRUE love, the eyes of Jesus. I have a feeling that everything around His face grew blurry and dim and the sound of the crowd was muffled by His voice. But what about her own thoughts?

What if she got up and walked away experiencing and having knowledge of God's love, but never agreeing to the point of loving herself? It would be so sad if this story had ended with her standing up and saying, "Look Jesus, I can see that You love me, I mean, no one has ever looked at me the way You are looking at me. No one has ever stood up for me like You are, or made me feel so valued. I see that You find me worthy of life and I believe you. However, I just don't agree that I am lovable or worthy of life." Is it possible that she could walk away, free from the stones of the people, but still stone herself on a daily basis? YES AND YES! In fact, I would venture to say that is the case with many of you reading this book! It is possible to be reconciled with God, but not be reconciled with yourself.

SELF-RECONCILIATION

OK, so let me make this clear. God speaks a Truth about you, and you can have knowledge about that Truth and even agree that God thinks about you and feels that way toward you, but if you don't align your thoughts and think that way yourself, then you are not reconciled. We know that God's love for us is not in question, the question is will we agree and love ourselves the way He loves us? This is often most challenging within ourselves, which is why self-reconciliation is so imperative. Our ministry to God should automatically lend itself to a new perspective, like the woman who anointed the feet of Jesus gained a new perspective of herself. From His throne room, we get a view from His heart and gain an appreciation of who we are. The love exchange shifts our heart and we see ourselves the way He does. This was why the psalmist was able to confidently proclaim...

"I will praise You for I am fearfully and wonderfully made;

*marvelous are your works, and THAT MY SOUL knows very well."
Psalm 139:14 (emphasis mine)*

He is not declaring that his spirit knows this, but rather his soul... meaning his mind, will, and emotions know WELL the beauty of who he is. The word "know" in this verse comes from the Hebrew word "yada," which includes the idea of being acquainted intimately. It is the same Hebrew word that is used in Genesis 4:1 that reads: "Adam knew Eve his wife; and she conceived..." That is an intimate acquaintance. It means *to be one with* or *to become as one.* The soul of the psalmist was intimately acquainted with the spirit and became as one. He was completely reconciled...not just vertically, but within himself as well.

Read Colossians 2:6-10 again...
"As you therefore have received Christ Jesus the Lord, so walk in Him, rooted and built up in Him and established in the faith, as you have been taught, abounding in it with thanksgiving. Beware lest anyone cheat you through philosophy and empty deceit, according to the tradition of men, according to the basic principles of the world, and not according to Christ. For in Him dwells all the fullness of the Godhead bodily; and you are complete in Him, who is the head of all principality and power." Colossians 2:6-10

These verses emphasize that we need to be intentional to stay rooted in Christ. We should build ourselves up, encourage ourselves in HIM; sit at His feet and be established through our faith and outpouring of praises. In other words, we need to stay in a posture of worship to God, ministering to Him. This is how we prevent the captivity of the world's stuff and keep from getting sucked into the bottomless pit of its pressures and perceptions. This is how we prevent the captivity of our own "stuff" and keep from getting sucked into the bottomless pit of our own pressures and self-judgments. It is only in Him that you will find fulfillment and completion. Everything else will keep you enslaved, constantly looking for more. God says we are complete in Him. We are filled up, made full, filled to the brim, abounding, liberally supplied, lacking nothing and rendered full. You know how you can tell when something is full? When it starts to overflow! But this overflowing fullness is only found in Him. This is what brought the psalmist self-reconciliation. He was rooted in and built up in God. How do I know? Just read through the Psalms!

RECONCILING YOUR REFLECTION

When I look into a mirror, I typically do so with the intention of seeing what I look like. I have in my mind what I think I look like, but the mirror reflects truth. It also gives me the opportunity to reconcile what I think I look like with what I really look like. But if I look at myself thinking I have everything in place, yet see that the mirror reflects something out of place, I have a problem. My two images (the one in my head and the one in the mirror) are not reconciled, meaning they are not congruous. So it is with the Word of God.

The Bible says it is like a mirror that reflects the truth. As I look into it, I will discover places where the image I have of myself is different than the image I see of myself in Scripture. You see, God's face is the perfect mirror; it reveals our TRUE reflection. Since we are created in His image, we find out what we look like as we look at Him. The more we peer at Him, the more we will see what should be and therefore, what is out of place in our lives; body and soul.

A natural mirror is not used for the purpose of simply reflecting your flaws; it is used to improve yourself. The intent of its use is to provide us with the opportunity to look our best. So the word of God is used to illuminate areas that are not in alignment with God's image; places where we have not reconciled with His nature in us. It shows us thoughts, feelings, and perceptions that we have, choices that we make that simply don't reflect His Word. However, when we only purpose to use the Word for revealing sin, we miss the motive or intent of love behind it. It is God's provision for the opportunity to BE your best!

"For if anyone is a hearer of the word and not a doer, he is like a man observing his natural face in a mirror; for he observes himself,

goes away, and immediately forgets what kind of man he was. But he who looks into the perfect law of liberty and continues in it, and is not a forgetful hearer but a doer of the work, this one will be blessed in what he does." James 1:23-25

To walk away from a mirror and not take advantage of the opportunity to improve your looks is choosing to make no change, even though you may see the need. It is not for lack of knowledge. This is what it means to simply hear the Word, but not DO the Word. It is like seeing the need for change, but choosing not to. Some of us will simply rely on the knowledge of our image, but do nothing to bring ourselves INTO the image!

"...you have put on the new man who is renewed in the knowledge according to the image of Him..." Colossians 3:10

Our new man is renewed, meaning "caused to grow up or changed into" in Greek as we grow in our knowledge of His image. So when you see your image through Him, you must reconcile the areas in your life that don't line up with what He says about you.

I often have my clients state truths while staring at themselves in the mirror. It is amazing how many of them simply cannot do it. I can ask them if they believe they are created with purpose, to be beautiful, and to be loved. I ask if they can boldly declare that they are loved, accepted, forgiven, redeemed, and no longer guilty. If they are believers, they will undoubtedly say yes to all the above. I will then hand them a mirror and ask them to speak those truths to themselves while looking at their reflection. That is when I see sweat begin to form and legs begin to shake. Why is it that we can say it is true, but there is a disconnect when it comes to actually receiving it? I guess we think it is because God is God so He HAS to forgive us, or He HAS to love us, or of course He thinks we are beautiful. But if I can't look into the reflection He has given me, and say those things to myself, then I am not in agreement, and I am not self-reconciled. I am not seeing myself the way God sees me, furthermore, I do not love myself the way God loves me.

DAVID AND ABSOLOM

We all hear about David and how he was a man after God's own heart and found favor in the sight of God" (Acts 7:46), however, there were some places in his life that were less than perfect and left unreconciled. Because of that we see years of cause and effect come to play.

Recall the storyline from 2 Samuel, chapters 11 & 12 where David falls into sexual sin with another man's wife, Bathsheba, and then has the man murdered by putting him on the front line of battle. When confronted, David repented and reconciled his sin before God.

"I have sinned against the Lord." 2 Samuel 12:13

Although David was in agreement with God that he had sinned, the outcome of this sin is that the son who had been illegitimately conceived was not to live. David fasted and prayed in hopes to change God's mind. The Bible says he lay on the ground and would not eat or be lifted up (2 Samuel 12:17). However, upon the death of the child, David's demeanor was lifted.

"So David arose from the ground, washed and anointed himself, and changed his clothes; and he went into the house of the Lord and worshiped." 2 Samuel 12:20

We see here that David was at peace with the consequences of his sin. We also can read in Psalm 51 his prayer of repentance where he reconciles his actions with God.

"For I acknowledge my transgressions...Against You, You only, have I sinned, And done this evil in Your sight." Psalm 51:3&4

Years later, his daughter Tamar was raped by her step-brother, Amnon (2 Samuel 13:14). Absolom, Tamar's full brother found out and was filled with anger. No doubt he expected David, as the king and Tamar's father, to avenge the act, but David did nothing. So the mess begins. Absolom's outrage with Amnon and his father's apathy led to murder. Absolom wanted justice, so he plotted to have Amnon killed. After his murder, instead of having Absolom killed as per the law of the day, David simply had him exiled from the land. With Absolom gone, David's misery only grew as he "mourned for his son every day" (2 Samuel 13:37), thus showing the pain he endured due to a lack of reconciliation. Absolom, however, only grew more bitter. In his anger, he led a revolt to steal his father's throne from him. To make a long story short, Absolom, against David's wishes, ends up murdered. It was upon his death that David cried out:

"O my son Absolom, my son, my son Absolom- if only I had died in your place!" 2 Samuel 18:33

David cried out that he would have died instead of Absolom! He was in essence saying, "Take me, I am the one who deserves death." Why? I believe we see the lack of reconciliation in his heart. Not with God, but with himself. I believe that David did not deal with the sexual sin in his family because he had not reconciled his own sexual sin within himself. Thus he was unable to see himself favorably. Furthermore, the words he cried out were not favorable words, but rather words of death. He was filled with guilt and shame instead of the grace and forgiveness of God. God forgave him, but he didn't forgive himself. It is likely that in the lack of his self-reconciliation, he considered that to avenge Tamar's rape would have been a double standard. This trickled into a series of circumstances in which he turned a blind eye, leaving many things not reconciled; all spiraled off of that one spot of shame. David let his less-than-perfect past keep him stuck in passivity because he lived with self-blame. And this is the case for many of us. We receive the forgiveness of God, but then find ourselves guilty, even years later. This lack of self-reconciliation will keep us hostage to our pasts and unable to deal with today's realities. Many of us aren't wrestling with God, we are wrestling with ourselves.

INNER HEALING

Inner healing happens when God, via the Holy Spirit, searches the deep places within our own lives for the purpose of revealing places that are not reconciled. This is a technique that we use a lot in the counseling room and I have personally found it to be very effective. The idea is to let the Holy Spirit navigate the client through their past and reveal places that have not been dealt with and are not reconciled with God's truth. Unless these places are brought into alignment with God, we will not live according to the fullness of our God-potential. This will not only affect you, but it will affect your relationships with others.

Inner healing is when the Holy Spirit recalls a scenario in your life where an agreement was made with something other than His Truth. It identifies a time when the words someone spoke or a message that was conveyed to you has altered your own thoughts or feelings and you've allowed that perception to become your truth. Over time, the "truth" of that moment gains power over you and begins to define who you are. This is a problem because you allow yourself to be defined by a lie, and not God's Truth. Inner healing allows you to go back into that experience with the Holy Spirit and reframe that moment with God in the scene. It is like a "redo" in the Spirit. In doing so, His presence of Truth shifts how you now perceive that moment, and you can choose to change your mind to the Truth and reconcile that moment with yourself.

MY INNER HEALING

When I first wrote this message, God was walking me through of season of self-reconciliation. He was bringing me into a deeper level of loving myself, which I have now come to realize is a continual process. God is ever-increasing us and bringing us more and more into an understanding of our workmanship and our design.

I recall during this particular season the Lord bringing to mind a picture of myself that was hanging in the hall of the home where I grew up. In this picture, I was about seven and was one of four ballerinas; all wearing different colored tutus. (Mine was purple) Now, as the image of this picture was continually being brought up in my mind, I began to connect with the emotion and thoughts that were tied to that picture and the "ballerina experience" as a whole. My strongest emotion was one of disgust because even as a child I had hips. Yes, you heard me right...hips. I have a strong hourglass shape that was prevalent even as a 7-year old. The problem was, no one else had hips in my class, nor did any of the girls in this picture. To make matters worse, I recalled the first tutu that was ordered was too small and one had to be specially made to fit my unusually hippy shape. I will be honest and tell you that until the Holy Spirit was recalling this picture, I had never thought about this experience. However, in transparency, I will tell you that I have always felt my hips were wide and spent the majority of my life fussing about them and trying to find things that would accentuate them less. As an adult, I have a small waist that further accentuates my hourglass figure, and I have never liked it. I am just keeping it real here! I finally decided to allow the Holy Spirit to take me to that spot where I would stand in the hallway, looking at that picture and hating it. As I stood there in the Spirit, I knew that God was telling me I was perfectly made and that He intentionally formed my hips with His own hands. I knew this, but was conflicted in my heart. The Lord wrestled with me until I repented of my disagreement and internal vow I had made of "hating my own hips." He actually whispered into my heart, "Even then, you didn't fit the mold. A pattern was made just for you." You see, although I knew in mind that I was "fearfully and wonderfully made," my soul did not "know it very well." (Psalm 139:14) My soul came into an agreement with the beauty of my body and I reconciled my physique with God that day.

I cannot tell you how that inner healing of self-reconciling shifted how I feel about myself. I had no idea how much I was affected by believing that my hips were too big! If you want to hear the story in detail, you will have to download the audio of this message...but it is quite a comical story to hear how a 43 year-old woman wrestled to reconcile the size of her hips as a 7 year old. Telling the story brought out MUCH healing and self-reconciliation among the crowd that day.

PETER'S INNER HEALING

I believe John 21, when Jesus asks Peter three times, "Peter, do you love me?" is a great picture of inner healing. Jesus needed to restore Peter's assignment and his God-design, which required reconciling those three moments of his past. Three times Peter had denied Jesus after declaring that he would follow Jesus even unto death. Thus, after the death of Jesus, Peter went right back to his old identity, failing as a fisherman, foregoing the call of God. I am sure that Peter was convinced that his lack of faithfulness had disqualified him for the kingdom and that his assignment was no longer applicable. But Jesus, finding him in his old environment, inserted Himself into the scene and began to work a Holy redo of Peter's denials...all three of them! You see, Jesus didn't want Peter's denials to define his future. Those moments were facts that he had lived, but they were not his Truth! Peter's own words of denial could not trump Jesus's words of acceptance.

"And I also say to you that you are Peter, and on this rock I will build My church, and the gates of Hades shall not prevail against it." Matthew 16:18

This was Peter's purpose and unless he reconciled his failures and agreed with his God design, his ministry to others would have never been possible. He had to forgive himself and love himself before he could love others the way God would. This is why self-reconciliation is so important.

JESUS'S SELF-RECONCILIATION

Even Jesus had moments when He had to reconcile His purpose. We see this in the Garden of Gethsemane when He reasoned with God about the cup He would need to bear. Although He knew the plan of God and the outcome, in His humanness, He had to reconcile His will with God's will.

"He knelt down and prayed, saying, "Father, if it is Your will take this

cup away from Me; nevertheless not My will, but Yours, be done."
Then an angel appeared to him from heaven, strengthening Him.
And being in agony, He prayed more earnestly. Then His sweat
became like great drops of blood falling down to the ground."
Luke 22:41-43

This is a serious moment of reasoning where Jesus was, in a sense, saying, "Father, if there is a plan B, I would like to choose it now." I love that we get to see how, much like us, even Jesus had to choose to align His will with God's; He was not coerced or forced to submit, but rather He chose to surrender. However, this process of aligning His will with God's was agonizing, to the point of sweating drops of blood. Boy, can I relate to that! But I am encouraged to read that Jesus was able to reconcile this with the help of an angel that came and ministered strength to Him. In the midst of His prayer, His ministry to God, this angel was released.

I am also reminded of Jesus on the cross when He cried out, "My God, my God, why have You forsaken Me?" (Matthew 27:46) Again we see that Jesus wrestled with the soul and the need to continuously reconcile His emotions with the will of God. While He was absolutely 100% God, He was also 100% man. These moments reveal how He had to contend with the flesh and practice reconciliation with the Father's will.

Jesus, Himself, proves that the flesh will war with the will of God. We can absolutely have knowledge of Truth, just as Jesus did; we can have verses embedded in our hearts, just as Jesus did; we can be reconciled with God, just as Jesus was, but still not have things reconciled within us. Jesus exemplified the process of self-reconciliation, showing us the importance of it. Had He not reconciled His purpose and the value of His assignment, we would not know life with God. Ultimately, it was through His own reconciliation that the world was reconciled to God! Jesus's own reconciliation demonstrated how self-reconciliation is a crucial piece in reconciliation with others.

MY SELF-RECONCILIATION

Let it be said that self-reconciliation is a process. God is forever transforming us into the image of Jesus (2 Corinthians 3:18), which means it is ongoing. We are constantly going to encounter areas in our lives where we wrestle with seeing ourselves the way God sees us. I have shared with you the changes that my marriage has gone through, but I would be remiss if I didn't share with you how I had to reconcile things within me before I could even begin to start reconciling things with Brad. One of the concepts that I wrestled with much of my life was the need to be pursued and loved. Because of the system that I was brought up in, I settled in the fact that God's love for me was enough and that I ought not have a desire for man's love. Not just from my husband, but from anyone. I reconciled God's love for me, but I actually used it as an excuse to not need any other love. In fact, I even convinced myself that it wasn't even a desire that I had. It was as if my need and desire for love from man was a sign of weakness, and a gap in my relationship with the Lord. However, if you would have asked me if this was a need that humans in general have, I would have said yes; that we must settle on God's love first, but then recognize the need to be loved by man as well. Remember, we are created for connection! I guess I thought I was an exception to this. In reality, I struggled with rejection, and so if I never desired or allowed myself to be loved, I would never be rejected. It was my way of guarding my heart. I would love others, with no expectation of any love in return. It was safe, but there was no love exchange. While this is a healthy mindset for some relationships, it is not a healthy mindset for all of your relationships, especially not in your marriage! My fear of being loved by Brad inadvertently kept me from connecting with him on a vulnerable level. It was not until I self-reconciled that God had designed me to be loved, more specifically from my husband, that I could begin to fight for it. You see I believed that God saw my design for love, but I didn't see it in myself. I was misaligned with God's truth and it hindered my marriage.

On the other side of this, Brad always wrestled with the expression of love. While he loves deeply, his "system" never showed or expressed love. He rarely even spoke the words, "I love you." At the root of this was the same fear of rejection that I had.

He felt that the expression of love was vulnerable and that it required letting down his guard. He often excused his lack of expression by resolving that he just wasn't a "romantic guy." To avoid feeling rejected by lack of expression, I chose to believe that he wasn't romantic. This was to reconcile the thought that I was simply not worth romancing. Plus, my system taught me that you should accept people and love them where they are, and just pray for the changes you desire. Again, there is a level of truth to that, but sometimes we take it too far. We use it as an excuse to keep us from God's most excellent design for relationship. Such was the case in our marriage.

I am sure that you can see how our own strongholds and lack of self-reconciliation kept us both in positions of fear and rejection. Brad also had to self-reconcile that God had designed him to love, more specifically his wife, before he could fight for it.

This is actually where the name of this book came from! Brad struggled "to love" and I struggled "to be loved." We realized that these fears actually trickled into many of our relationships. These truths are a crucial part of God's design for us and key to establishing healthy relationships. We also realized that just because we had a particular nature, that it should not excuse us from coming into and reconciling with the nature of God. Brad realized that since God is a romantic, he must have romance within him. He learned that by watching how God romanced His people as His Beloved, that Brad could learn how to do the same with me. He reconciled that if God is a romantic, then God's romance was in him.

There will be no freedom in your relationships until you see yourself the way God sees you. This is more than believing what God thinks about you, it is thinking it yourself. It is so easy to say what we know God says about us, but it is a whole other level to say it about yourself and to yourself. Just like David, if we don't reconcile within us, forgiving ourselves, loving ourselves, seeing our value and pressing on toward our calling, then we will stay stuck in our "less than" image and hold ourselves captive to our own limited opinion. It is time that we, as a people of God, reconcile with ourselves the truth of John 17:22 when Jesus said to God, "And the glory that you gave Me I have given them..."

I agree with Jesus, I am glorious. You also are glorious, so release yourself from the thoughts that keep you from walking in that confidence and fall in love with you!

PRAYER PRACTICE

God, I thank You for the ways You have healed me on the inside. That you find places deep within me where I have not aligned myself with You. I love the way You gently search me and seek me and see if there be an offense in me and that You are unwilling for there to be any spot or wrinkle. What a great God You are, that even things that would seem irrelevant and insignificant, You deal with. Thank You for desiring the purest of me; past, present, and future.

In Jesus' name I pray, Amen.

Chapter 16
Ministering to You

Walking in self-reconciliation includes ministering to yourself. The world calls this "self-care." As you start reconciling within yourself the worth you find in Christ, you will organically start to tend to yourself better.

I think that in our attempts to put others first, we too often sacrifice what is best for us in the process. I counsel and coach people daily who constantly abandon their own hula-hoops. They let go of their own needs, their own opinions, and their own thoughts and practically lose themselves in service to others. One common example is seen with women who have children and are married. They sacrifice their sleep, their time, their meals, their friendships, their dreams, etc. And while I absolutely know that having a family requires sacrifice, I see it taken to the point of losing their identity outside of their home.

Now, I was a stay at home mom for years, and that was the choice that we made. It required putting my education on hold, my career on hold, and sacrificing a lot of other things to raise our children and homeschool them. This was not bad, but where I struggled was in maintaining a sense of self outside of my children and my husband and their needs and dreams. Everything I did centered on them and I had to fight to hold on to things that were "just for me." Things like working out, singing in a music ministry, and teaching in church. There were times and seasons when the needs of family required some shifting, but if I went too long not fulfilling some of my own desires, I grew pretty bitter. My tendency to be a "Martha" resulted in the same troublesome spirit that plagued Martha. On top of that, I had to contend with the opinion of my system that told me that motherhood was all about sacrificing your life and that being a wife meant living my life around my husband's schedule and fitting my dreams into his (or rather, give up my own dreams to support his.)

Again, I want to be careful here, this book is not about giving you a reason to abandon your duties, but rather it is about empowering you to set healthy boundaries that guard your "lot." We must keep capacity in our lives for us! This means spirit, soul and body.

"Now may the God of peace Himself sanctify you completely; and may your whole spirit, soul and body be preserved blameless at the coming of our Lord Jesus Christ." 1 Thessalonians 5:23

"Beloved, I pray that all may go well with you and that you may be in good health, as it goes well with your soul." 1 John 1:2 (ESV)

"I have set the Lord always before me; Because He is at my right hand I shall not be moved. Therefore my heart is glad, and my glory rejoices; My flesh also will rest in hope." Psalm 16:8-9

It is clear that there is more than just our ministry to God that is important. There are many places throughout the Scripture that talk specifically about ministering to our own soul and body as well. Not only that, but it is clear that the health of each of them directly affects the health of the others. In other words, our ministry to God will directly affect the way we minister to our soul and our body, and vice versa. As we minister to our souls and physical bodies, the more it will positively affect our ministry to God. This is why there must be an element of all three when establishing personal health and wholeness, however, the foundation and root is your ministry to God. That being said, let's break down the care of your soul and your body, but remember, in many ways they intertwine.

SOUL CARE

Tending to your soul should be a regular practice. The soul includes your thoughts, your emotions, and your will. In the counseling room, I call these the thinker, the feeler, and the picker. In short, your soul is your personality; it is the core of who you are and how God designed you in order to fit His assignment for your life. Every one of us has thoughts, feelings, and desires and to deny them is to ignore part of how you are created. It is good to identify what you think, how you feel, and what you want and it is unhealthy to simply ignore the soul. However, caring for your soul means being self-aware and then intentionally choosing to navigate your thinker, feeler, and picker towards the spirit. This means dragging your soul into alignment with the Spirit of God. This is how you self-reconcile...you bring every thought/emotion captive to the Truth.

"For though we walk in the flesh, we do not war according to the flesh. For the weapons of our warfare are not carnal but mighty in God for pulling down strongholds, casting down arguments and every high thing that exalts itself against the knowledge of God, bringing every thought into captivity to the obedience of Christ"
2 Corinthians 10:3-5

Through the Word you can be sure that your personality, meaning your thinker, feeler, and picker, is motivated by the Holy Spirit and not your flesh.

"For the word of God is living and powerful, and sharper that any two-edged sword, piercing even to the division of soul and spirit, and of joint and marrow, and is a discerner of the thoughts and intents of the heart." Hebrews 4:12

The Word will help you discern what is of your own flesh and what is of God. It has the ability to divide your soul AND body from the spirit, exposing where you do not line up with the Father. Sometimes we feel something or are convinced of something and it seems to be so right, however, if it doesn't agree with the Word, it is simply not right. This can be things within your heart, mind, or even your physical body. This is why ministering the Word to yourself every day is so important. It is how you learn to discern truth within yourself. It helps cut away the selfish parts and whittle out the God-design, which is found somewhere in the middle of all your thoughts and emotions!

"Therefore lay aside all filthiness and overflow of wickedness, and receive with meekness the implanted word, which is able to save your soul." James 1:21

The selfish tendencies of the soul are rescued and sanctified by the Word of God. Again, this is why ministering the Word to your soul is so important. It is by the Word that your soul is trained towards righteousness and "shaped up" for your God-assignment.

"All Scripture is given by inspiration of God, and is profitable for doctrine, for reproof, for correction, for instruction in righteousness, that the man of God may be complete, thoroughly equipped for every good work." 2 Timothy 3:16-17

The Message says it like this...

"Every part of Scripture is God-breathed and useful one way or another—showing us truth, exposing our rebellion, correcting our mistakes, training us to live God's way. Through the Word we are put together and shaped up for the tasks God has for us."

It is important that we are intentional to guard and care for our soul. Part of this means speaking biblical truths into our own selves about who we are and the way God designed us. I know we have spent much of this book talking about healing in your soul and self-reconciliation. But let me reiterate that it is also good to tend to your own thoughts, feelings, and desires, meaning spend time caring for them. Your design is woven into your personality. Even what would be considered your greatest personality weakness will become your greatest personality strength when the Holy Spirit navigates it.

"And He said to me, 'My grace is sufficient for you, for My strength is made perfect in weakness.' Therefore most gladly I will rather boast

in my infirmities, that the power of Christ may rest upon me. Therefore I take pleasure in infirmities, in reproaches, in needs, in persecutions, in distresses, for Christ's sake. For when I am weak, then I am strong." 2 Corinthians 12:9-10

We ought not despise our weaknesses or try to squelch them, but rather bring them under the submission of the Holy Spirit. Somewhere in the midst of all that "messy flesh" is a God-design that is perfect and beautiful. This means your passion for your assignment is found in your emotions; your wisdom for your assignment is found in your mind; and your unction to navigate toward your assignment is found in your will. So you must not dismiss your soul. Instead, feed it the Word of God and train it to flow with the current of the Holy Spirit. The Word will cause your soul to be picked up by His current; I call this the power of the Drift...with a capital "D."

> *"The king's heart is in the hand of the Lord,*
> *Like the rivers of water;*
> *He turns it wherever He wishes."*
> *Proverbs 21:1*

Soul-care ensures that your dreams and passions are not stolen from you. Your purpose was knit in you in your mother's womb and you carry it in your heart (Psalm 139). This is why we must be good stewards and pay attention to what is within.

GUARDING YOUR HEART

"Keep your heart with all diligence, For out of it spring the issues of life." Proverbs 4:23

A garden starts out with just seeds in the ground. In order for those seeds to grow into a healthy harvest without any bugs, weeds, or rotting, a farmer must tend to it; he must care for it and cultivate it if he wants to get the greatest return. Just as a farmer is given the responsibility to keep his garden, so we are to keep our hearts. We have the seed of God's purpose within, but if we don't tend to it and cultivate it, neither will it produce the best and healthiest fruit, which is His will for our lives. "To keep" also means *to guard*, which means God is giving you the duty of guarding your God-design, which is seeded inside of you.

I have heard it said that to come into salvation is to win the heart. But the challenge comes after salvation when we need to keep the heart. You see, while only God can win the heart, He invites us to partner with Him by giving us the stewardship of keeping the heart. This is because the enemy comes to steal, kill, and destroy us (John10:10), but once we come into salvation, since he can no longer have us, he goes after our dreams! He knows that "a people without a vision will perish" and will lose heart for life.

"Where there is no revelation, the people cast off restraint..."
Proverbs 29:18

We have all heard the term "losing heart." We use this phrase to mean one is discouraged or has stopped believing that she can accomplish her dreams, or her God-assignment. It is when you lose the unction of the Holy Spirit to chase after your dreams and this happens when you don't keep your heart with all diligence. It is interesting to note that the Hebrew word for *diligence* actually denotes the idea of *placing in confinement, to guard, or to imprison.* This is a serious guarding of the heart; diligent to the point of keeping your dreams and passions under lock and key. This is the whole point of setting healthy boundaries; to guard your God-design and keep it locked in your heart. We must not let our hearts be taken, stolen, squelched, or shut down. And we must not give them away either. Loving and treasuring your own design will keep you from allowing this in your life. This is why loving you is so important. We keep things we treasure under lock and key because we highly value them and we do not want them taken from us. But too often our system will tell us that we aren't worth guarding our hearts or that we should sacrifice for the sake of others...again I say, not at the expense of losing your own design!

MY LOSS OF HEART

I have shared much with you about my own season of healing when I came to a place of deep dissatisfaction in my marriage. Let me go back to that season and share with you what I was going through personally. The longing I experienced was not just because of the loss of passion in my marriage; it was also that I had lost passion in my own life. Recall the question the Lord asked me about my first love and how it revealed that I had strayed from my first ministry to Him. If that wasn't enough of a paradigm shift, I also felt the Lord shift His focus to me and the passion I had for myself and my own dreams. I was beginning to feel a spirit of depression and a general lack of zeal in my heart and mind. Somewhere in the midst of discovering all of this, I decided I needed to seek some counsel. Because of what I do, I thought it was best to seek the help of someone outside of my ministry; I needed someone who didn't know me. Upon meeting my counselor, I began to tell her what I did and what my life looked like. As she asked questions about what I wanted or desired, I noticed that I had a hard time answering them. I was so trained to CHOOSE what was right and the right way to feel, and the right way to think, that I was totally dismissing my own desires and thoughts to the point that I had lost touch with what was really in my heart; I was losing touch with me. My life had become all about living for the needs and desires of others: my husband, my kids, my family, my clients, the residents in our home, my staff, our volunteers, etc. I poured into them, served them, celebrated them, and was at their disposal. I simply had no time and no energy left for me, and I had no time to even consider how I felt about anything. But the worst part was that over the years, due to my system, I had concluded that it didn't matter anyway because I just needed to "put others first."

My first assignment from my new counselor was to make a list of my deepest desires and my deepest needs. At first, I was resistant because I didn't feel that spending time exploring my desires was biblical (crazy!), but this was about the time that God revealed to me that His purpose for me was woven into my heart and mind, and that His seed of unction was inside of me and I needed to get in touch with it. Here is what I discovered. The majority of my desires, such as to be loved, to be romanced, to be celebrated, to write books, or to empower people, was a part of my God-design. Furthermore, I noticed that there was a huge overlap in what was a desire and what was a need. Our Creator created us with a need to be loved, and religion had taught me to give up the right to be loved. I distinctly remember the day that I made that vow, and I am quite certain this was the day that my heart disconnected from Brad's. In my attempt to seek a way to manage the feeling of rejection of not being loved in my marriage, I shut down my heart and the vulnerability that is required to connect and be loved. I can only assume that this is when I shifted from feeling like his wife to simply feeling like his "maid, secretary, and sex-mate." Through this, I somehow came to believe that my role as a wife was simply functional. But I also felt this way in many areas of my life; I just functioned, as I needed to. Simply said, I had lost my passion *for* life to the *duties* of life. In doing so, I lost connection with who I was and the desires of my own heart. I had lost connection with me.

In the midst of prioritizing the needs and desires of others, I slipped in my own self-care, which ultimately had an affect on my physical well-being. All of these revelations led me to the process of redefining my ministry to God, my ministry to self, and my ministry to others. This season is actually what inspired this book!

PRIORITIZING YOU

I know that it is hard to prioritize you when it comes to self-care. Somehow, we have bought into the lie that it is selfish to say no to others and say yes to ourselves. But that part of ministering to you requires self-care. The way you tend to your soul will directly affect your body and vice versa. This means that sometimes tending to your mind means getting more rest, taking a nap, eating better, or cutting things out of your schedule so you can think straight. How you care for your physical body will absolutely impact the way you think and how you feel. We all know this, yet we struggle to practice it and prioritize our own physical health.

I cannot tell you how many women I minister to who are literally ragged from giving their lives away. They are tired, grouchy, and bitter. Most of them are angry with their husbands and struggle to keep their kids and house in order. Their solution? To either work harder and do more, thus exhausting themselves, or give up and do nothing, thus settling in defeat. Neither of these are God's solution. God wants you to set healthy boundaries and prioritize your own needs because you are worth it, remember? This is why the chapter about falling in love with you came before this chapter; you must have a respect for your own design if you are going to be able to prioritize the needs of your design.

BODY CARE

A large part of prioritizing you means tending to your body. This means physically taking care of you. Every body has needs; some of these needs are emotional, some are mental, and some are purely physical. But they are all intertwined. This means if you only minister to your soul, then your self-ministry is incomplete. Just as the priests tended to the temple, so we must also tend to our temples, which is our physical body. After all, we are hosting the King of Kings via the Holy Spirit in our bodies!

"Do you not know that you are the temple of God and that the Spirit of God dwells in you? If anyone defiles the temple of God, God will destroy him. For the temple of God is holy, which temple you are."
1 Corinthians 3:16-17

"Or do you not know that your body is the temple of the Holy Spirit who is in you, whom you have from God, and you are not your own? For you were bought at a price; therefore glorify God in your body and in your spirit, which are God's."
1 Corinthians 6:19-20

Coming to the understanding that your physical body literally houses the Holy Spirit should cause you to want to take care of it. We are not machines; we are physical beings with physical needs.

175

We see evidence of God's care for the body throughout the Scriptures. Think with me for a moment about when Elijah was dismayed and depressed in the wilderness. He had just experienced a huge victory standing up against the prophets of Baal. After that, he immediately entered in to intercession, warring for rain to come and end the drought. He had been in a season of battling and pressed in until he got a breakthrough. No doubt, after the long battles, he was exhausted. No wonder when he faced the threats of Jezebel, he was simply unable to continue in his stance. Maybe it was just too much, he had had enough and he was simply tired and weary from battling. Scripture doesn't poignantly say, but we can infer through the text.

"But he himself went a day's journey into the wilderness, and came and sat down under a broom tree. And he prayed that he might die, and said, 'It is enough! Now, Lord, take my life, for I am no better than my fathers!'

"Then as he lay and slept under a broom tree, suddenly an angel touched him, and said to him, 'Arise and eat.' Then he looked, and there by his head was a cake baked on coals, and a jar of water. So he ate and drank, and lay down again. And the angel of the Lord came back the second time, and touched him, and said, 'Arise and eat, because the journey is too great for you.' So he arose, and ate and drank; and he went in the strength of that food forty days and forty nights as far as Horeb, the mountain of God." 1 Kings 19:4-8

Many things were needed in Elijah's soul to shake him out of his fear and depressive mentality, but before God addressed that, he addressed the needs of his body...sleep, rest, water, food, and refreshment; not just once, but twice! And He addressed these needs in the wilderness, a place afforded to Elijah to simply retreat and get away. God indeed does end up pulling Elijah out of his depression by telling him to get up and move forward (1 Kings 19:9-16), but not without tending to his physical needs first! He never dismisses the needs of the body and importance of tending to those needs.

176

We could learn a lot from this—the power of sleep, rest, water, food, and silence. The opportunity for God to touch us is often found by simply stopping and being still; getting away from the busyness of life and allowing our bodies to be cared for holds much power and importance in the kingdom.

Even Jesus Himself was intentional to get away and tend to His own need for rest. He was intentional to provide food for the multitude and uses the story of the Good Samaritan, a man who tended to the physical needs of another, as an example of what it looks like to love your neighbor. In most cases in the gospels, Jesus ministers to the physical body before He even reveals His identity and it was through His practical ministry to the physical needs of the people that they were won over. God cares and is deeply concerned about our physical well-being.

CARING FOR ME

I shared with you earlier in this chapter about my loss of heart and how I had lost touch with why I do what I do and what my desires were. For 15 years, I struggled with managing the many duties of motherhood and still finding time to self-care. But when I stepped into ministry, the many burdens and duties only increased. I worked so hard to be everything to everyone. Never wanting to disappoint anyone (mostly myself), I would rarely say no, unless it was literally impossible to do what was asked. I am a doer, so I would just get up earlier, work harder, move faster and stay up later to get it all done. Well, guess what? I ended up getting sick. At first, it was just emotionally and mentally that I struggled, but I was "wise and spiritually mature enough" to push through that. HA! I would often sacrifice my own quiet time to minister to others, I would skip my workouts to handle a walk-in client, and I would stay up late praying with someone over the phone. Not only did I lose heart in the midst of all this, I lost my physical strength.

Now, this is where I must tell you that I believe the body will always mimic the soul. So just as I was wasting away emotionally and mentally, my body followed suit. Much of this was due to poor choices, even though they were choices that I thought were right at the time. I was living according to my system and not to my ministry to God. Somewhere in the midst of my marital challenges, the visits to my counselor, and the depression that I was warring with, I started having physical manifestations. My hair was falling out (in chunks), my nails were splitting, I struggled to stay awake throughout the day, yet I could never get into a deep sleep at night. My body ached constantly, and when I woke up in the morning my head felt like it weighed one hundred pounds. I was continuously on the verge of tears and internally felt panicked quite a bit. For the most part I was able to press through a lot of the mental and emotional part of this, but physically, I was literally falling apart. If you know me, I am highly energetic and I rarely get sick; and when I do, I just drink more water and press through it. I am one that tells my body what to do and then I move on. But this was different! And God was NOT going to let me move forward. I was in a holding pattern with my body and it was SO frustrating.

After a year of seeing a dietician, working with a trainer, and seeing a gynecologist, I was diagnosed with Stage 3 adrenal fatigue. In short, my adrenal glands were so worn out from producing cortisol constantly to keep up with my lifestyle that they simply stopped producing. I am not sure if you know how important your adrenals are, or all that cortisol does for you, but suffice it to say, it is a vital part of living. I had no fight or flight reaction, which not only left me feeling continuously flat, but I wouldn't even flinch as I watched a bowl fall from the top of the cabinet and hit me square in the face.

I was told that the healing process for this stage was about 18-24 months AT BEST. Well, I wasn't going to receive that, I immediately began to minister healing to my body and receive prayer for healing. I expected God to speed up my process! However, not a month into this, I heard the Lord very clearly say, "Lisa, I am going to take my time healing you." I was bugged by this response, but when I sought the Lord in regard, I began to understand. You see, God was teaching me the importance of establishing healthy habits with boundaries that would guard my physical well-being. He wanted me to learn how to set a pace to navigate my health and energy better. I needed to learn to prioritize me. Furthermore, I sensed that He was telling me that this was a vital step in preparing me for where He plans to take me.

I spent no less than a year changing my diet, drinking more water, disciplining myself to go to bed by 10 pm, and shutting my eyes for at least 20 minutes every afternoon. "Daily siesta" was on my calendar for 3:00 pm every day, so that no one would schedule any appointments for me. It was challenging for me to stop in the middle of my day to turn off my office lights, shut my blinds, TURN OFF MY PHONE, and close my eyes... but at this point, I couldn't afford not to. It was a very long and frustrating season. I had never experienced the feeling of not being able to just push through, but my body just couldn't do anymore. My body and my soul were weary and I needed rest.

"Come to Me, all you who labor and are heavy laden, and I will give you rest. Take my yoke upon you and learn from Me, for I am gentle and lowly in heart and you will find rest for your souls. For My yoke is easy and My burden is light." Matthew 11:28-30

This passage never resonated with me as deeply as it did through that season. Through it, God gave me the antidote to discovering and reaping the ease of life. I needed to COME to Him and yoke myself to Him; this means to connect and attach my heart to His heart, and learn from Him, not from my system. Furthermore, it was through my connection to Him that I was able to re-connect with me. The yoke of the Lord truly is easy, which means "benevolent, kindly, and fitting" in the Greek language. He will not call you into something that doesn't benefit you or extend His kindness to you or that goes against the core of who you are and your design. To find yourself feeling anything less is to be yoked with things other than God.

Although I am on the other side of this adrenal fatigue, I still have just enough symptoms here and there to remind me to guard my newfound healthy habits and stay yoked to God. It is not popular among many sects to guard you. It will irritate others whose guilt will try to suck you into being a "Martha." I even had a lady reprove me after I shared during a message that I had said "no" to ministering to a walk-in client to make my appointment at the gym with my trainer. Without context, I can understand why someone might look upon that poorly, but I had shared this within the context of my own story. Yet this poor woman still felt that I should have, and STILL should, "prioritize people over my workouts." What she was not getting is that I am not prioritizing my workouts; I am prioritizing *me*!

I have learned over these past few years to do for myself what I was so passionate about teaching others to do for themselves. Because of that, my ministry to others is no longer about *doing*; it is about *being*. I focus on God by connecting with Him and His nature first. Out of that I get connected with me and who I am in Christ; my God-design. I have grown in my love for my purpose and the beauty of it. I understand and appreciate the uniqueness of my personality and how God created me to fit that purpose.

People may think it is selfish when you tend to yourself and care for your own needs, however, you must realize the impact your health and wholeness has on yourself and on the lives of those around you. Not taking care of you will result in not feeling your best and ultimately will hinder you from BEING your best. In reality, a healthier you makes for healthier relationships! Remember, we will only love our neighbor AS we love ourselves.

❧PRAYER PRACTICE

God, I thank You for the gift of life. Thank You for teaching me the importance of taking care of myself and for empowering me to guard my own mind, heart, and body. Continue to show me how to prioritize myself so that I can be the best me You have in mind. I know that You have an assignment for me and I do not want to wear out before I accomplish all You have given me to do. I thank You for the wisdom to set boundaries and for the courage to say no!

In Jesus' name I pray, Amen.

Part 3
Others

Chapter 17
Loving Others

So let's review this whole section for a moment and see how God has positioned us to view loving others. We spent many chapters discussing the importance of connection with God and establishing a healthy relationship with Him first. Then we discussed the importance of connecting with ourselves and walking in personal heath; spirit, soul, and body. Without looking at these two relationships, God and self, you would not be positioned to succeed in your relationships with others. Again, this seems backwards from what we have been taught, but it is so empowering because it gives you authority over your own life. This means that you don't HAVE to be controlled by horizontal relationships, and though they absolutely may affect you, they do not define you. You are defined first by your connection with God and your self-connection. The more you connect with God through your ministry to Him, the more you will come to know who He is and His nature. This is ultimately where you learn what love looks like; it is found in His nature.

HIS GLORY
The glory of the Lord is the nature or the character of God. It is the knowledge of who He is. In Exodus, when Moses asked to see the glory of the Lord, the Lord actually covered his face so that Moses SAW nothing. But he learned who God was.

"So it shall be, while My glory passes by, that I will put you in the cleft of the rock, and will cover you with My hand while I pass by." Exodus 33:22

"And the Lord passed before him, and proclaimed, 'The Lord, the Lord God, merciful and gracious, longsuffering, and abounding in

goodness and truth.'" Exodus 34:6

You see, the glory is the person of God. It wasn't until Jesus came that we saw what the glory looked like in human form; He was the anointing of God; meaning He was the manifestation of the glory. Furthermore, He only functioned out of the glory, or the person, of God. Now, the person of God lives in you, His glory, via the Holy Spirit. Our ministry, much like the ministry of Jesus, should only flow out of that glory, or the person of God. The outcome that is seen or demonstrated by who we are is the anointing of God. It is the tangible movement of God's glory seen in the way we live our lives and our very being. This is why Jesus was referred to as "The Anointed One," because He was God made flesh and His very being made the glory of God visible to the world.

"And the Word became flesh and dwelt among us, and we beheld His glory, the glory as of the only begotten of the Father, full of grace and truth...No one has seen God at any time. The only begotten Son, who is in the bosom of the Father, He has declared Him" John 1:14 & 18

Before Jesus, God was a mystery. There was evidence of Him, and people certainly saw His works and learned His ways by His acts, but Jesus actually manifested the person of God in the flesh (1 Timothy 3:16).

We, too, are called to be the manifestation of the person God. He is to be manifested and made known to the world through us and the way we live our lives. This is what ministers to others. Our own knowledge of God and His love and our personal experiences with His love changes us (the way we see and love ourselves) and thus should alter the way we love others. I wish I could shorten this passage but to bring this point home, you MUST read it all!

"Beloved, let us love one another, for love is of God; and everyone who loves is born of God and knows God. He who does not love does not know God, for God is love. In this the love of God was manifested

toward us, that God has sent His only begotten Son into the world, that we might live through Him. In this is love, not that we loved God, but that He loved us and sent His Son to be the propitiation for our sins. Beloved, if God so loved us, we also ought to love one another.

"No one has seen God at any time. If we love one another, God abides in us, and His love has been perfected in us. By this we know that we abide in Him, and He in us, because He has given us of His Spirit. And we have seen and testify that the Father has sent the Son as Savior of the world. Whoever confesses that Jesus is the Son of God, God abides in him, and he in God. And we have known and believed the love that God has for us. God is love, and he who abides in love abides in God, and God in him.

"Love has been perfected among us in this: that we may have boldness in the day of judgment; because as He is, so are we in this world. There is no fear in love; but perfect love casts out fear, because fear involves torment. But he who fears has not been made perfect in love." 1 John 4:7-18

Crazy that this has brought us right back to one of the very first verses in this book. HIS perfected love in us will compel us to love others in a way that is healthy and without fear.

THE POWER OF GOD'S LOVE

It is only through the person of God in us that we will come to know what REAL love looks like; perfected love. More importantly, it is only through believing and receiving that love that we will be able to love others the same. But it is only His love that will truly minister to others with power. I think we get too focused on what ministry *looks like* and forget that it simply *looks like* His love. Not worldly love, but His supernatural love. In fact, the Bible reminds us that to minister without His love amounts to nothing; it will have no affect.

"Though I speak with the tongues of men and of angels, but have

not love, I have become sounding brass or a clanging cymbal. And though I have the gift of prophecy, and understand all mysteries and all knowledge, and though I have all faith, so that I could remove mountains, but have not love, I am nothing. And though I bestow all my goods to feed the poor, and though I give my body to be burned, but have not love, it profits me nothing. 1 Corinthians 13:1-3

The word *profits* in Greek means *to prevail, better, or advantage.* You see, we can demonstrate all kinds of miraculous signs, like moving mountains, but if our actions are not rooted in love, then those signs will have no kingdom advantage.

They will not prevail, which means they will not prove more powerful than the opposing forces. Here is an example for you from Exodus.

"So Moses and Aaron went in to Pharaoh, and they did so, just as the Lord commanded. And Aaron cast down his rod before Pharaoh and before his servants, and it became a serpent.

"But Pharaoh also called the wise men and the sorcerers; so the magicians of Egypt, they also did in like manner with their enchantments. For every man threw down his rod, and they became serpents. But Aaron's rod swallowed up their rods." Exodus 7:10-12

Even man can display signs that are seemingly miraculous, and sometimes even are because of demonic forces. It is possible for me to demonstrate love from my soul, but if it isn't compelled by God's love, then it will not prevail, and will likely also wear me out. Aaron and Moses were compelled by the call of God. They understood their God-assignment and His love for them. Neither of them were confident in themselves apart from God, but their own knowledge of God's love for His people and for them motivated them. The sign that was displayed through Aaron's rod was rooted in God's glory, but the sign that was displayed through the magician's rod was rooted in man's glory, which is why it was defeated! Only the sign rooted in God's love prevailed!

We must not diminish the miraculous power of godly love.

Yes, His anointing is seen in signs, miracles, and wonders, but let's not limit that to just things like healing and deliverance. What about the miracle of loving the unlovable, or extending grace to the unforgiveable? Remember the anointing of God should flow out of His glory within us. He is absolutely a God of healing and deliverance, but He is first and foremost a God of love, and His love knows no bounds.

HIS PERFECT LOVE

God's love is not something that can be mustered up in your own strength. Simply said, His love, although seen through your actions, is not a matter of doing but a matter of being. I cannot emphasize this enough. God IS love (1 John 4:8), which means it is something you are. You ARE the essence of God's love and that love is seen through the way you live. But this action comes only as you abide in Him and His love (John 15). So let me be clear that love is something that you are (or become in Christ), and demonstrating that love is something that you do. One without the other is incomplete. You can have the glory of God in you, but it is of no value if you do not allow His glory to flow through you, which is His anointing. Conversely, to flow in what the anointing looks like without the root of His glory profits nothing.

God's love doesn't look like the world's love. We are not talking about "philos" (or brotherly) love. Philos love is the love that most of us as Christians practice for others, loving those whom we are connected to through fellowship and friendship.

We are also not talking about an "eros" (or erotic) love that is seen in intimate relationships, namely within marriage. These two loves are rooted in the soul, which means if they are navigated by the Holy Spirit, they can be good. However, they can also sour very quickly when the flesh navigates them. This is why they are not a perfect love, unless they are rooted in His "agape" love first.

The only love that is perfect is agape love, which is only found in God. Look at what an agape love looks like...

"Love suffers long and is kind; love does not envy; love does not

parade itself, is not puffed up; does not behave rudely, does not seek its own, is not provoked, thinks no evil; does not rejoice in iniquity, but rejoices in the truth; bears all things, believes all things, hopes all things, endures all things. Love never fails" 1 Corinthians 13:4-8

Read it in *The Voice* translation…

"Love is patient; love is kind. Love isn't envious, doesn't boast, brag, or strut about. There's no arrogance in love; it's never rude, crude, or indecent—it's not self-absorbed. Love isn't easily upset. Love doesn't tally wrongs or celebrate injustice; but truth—yes, truth—is love's delight! Love puts up with anything and everything that comes along; it trusts, hopes, and endures no matter what. Love will never become obsolete."

Sound familiar? Think back to Chapter 2 when I discussed God's design for healthy relationships. The things I listed are rooted in this passage about God's love.

I don't know about you, but this kind of love is impossible without God. It can't be found in our system or even in our own understanding, but rather it is only found in Him. It is only possible with God! Here is another beautiful description of God's love that illuminates how vastly different man's love is.

"The Lord is merciful and gracious,
Slow to anger, and abounding in mercy.
He will not always strive with us,
Nor will He keep His anger forever.
He has not dealt with us according to our sins,
Nor punished us according to our iniquities.
For as the heavens are high above the earth,
So great is His mercy toward those who fear Him…"
Psalm 103:8-11

Honestly, I could copy and paste hundreds of passages, but the fullness of His love cannot be explained, that is why it was demonstrated through the life of Jesus Christ.

This is the love needed when it comes to ministering to others. It is the love that honors God because it is about God, not about you or the people you are ministering to. I have made the mistake of loving others too much when I loved them more than I loved God. It was a devastating love that left me very wounded and rejected. I have also loved others too little when I loved without freedom and transparency, but in fear. God's love is perfect. It demonstrates not only in perfect ways, but also in perfect amounts. In truth, a small demonstration of God's love is more complete than a large demonstration of a fleshy or worldly love.

The only way to love others through His perfect love is to be saturated in His love first, which is His glory. This is why focusing on others is last in this book. Were it not for His glory in us, we would be unable to love others with a love that isn't of this world. Aren't you excited to know that you and I have a love capacity that is supernatural? We don't have to love the way we always have; we are empowered with a love that separates us from the world and ministers to others in ways we never could in our humanness.

PRAYER PRACTICE

Father, thank You for Your love and that You transform me daily by Your love. Thank You for the ease of simply sitting with You and being saturated by Your presence. I declare that Your love is my very being and that because of You I am oozing with a love that is not of this world...Your love. Your love brings balance, freedom, and effectiveness into my ministry and it is the answer to any question. Thank You that I don't have to have all the answers because I know You, and You are the answer to all things.

In Jesus' name I pray, Amen.

Chapter 18
Ministering to Others

Ministry to others is not about doing, it is a state of being. This means that WHO we are, the evidence of God in our lives, and the way we live our lives is what ministers to others. More than words that we speak and actions that we demonstrate, it is simply our state of being.

A RESIDENT'S TESTIMONY

I will never forget when I took one of our residents to a fundraiser to give her testimony. When she had finished sharing all the ways we had helped her, one person in the crowd asked her this question: "What would you say impacted you the most while at Crazy8?" She pondered for a moment and then said, "Well, I feel like I should say that they paid for my car repairs, or meeting with my counselor, but I don't think that's it." And then she paused and began to cry as she said, "It was their love. And not just their love for us, but the love we saw they had even for each other. It really wasn't so much about what they did for me, but how I got to see what true love looks like on a daily basis."

By no means do we have all the answers when it comes to the ladies and their children that we minister to, and we are often stumped on how to handle things. But we as a staff have resolved that love is the final answer and that we just need to be and not do. The glory of God that we carry releases the love that this resident experienced. But let me be sure to tell you that we also have to be intentional to walk in reconciliation with God and with ourselves. Otherwise, our own broken areas would skew our love for them, thus tainting our ministry to them.

FULL reconciliation with God and self is the key to ministering and loving others without fear of acceptance, perception, or judgment. You will no longer be concerned with what they think or how they respond, rather your focus will be on what you are called and compelled to do.

THE WOMAN AT THE WELL

Let's revisit the story of Jesus with the woman at the well from John 4. If you remember, in Chapter 1 of this book, we learned how connection requires transparency and vulnerability, and saw how Jesus connected with the woman in her most vulnerable spot, which was shame and guilt. I want you to note the reconciliation that takes place throughout the story. Because of Jesus's unconditional love for her, and His unwillingness to relent in connecting with her, she came into His love. She was reconciled with God. But we also see that she not only reconciled with God, she self-reconciled.

"The woman then left her waterpot, went her way into the city, and said to the men, 'Come see a Man who told me all things that I ever did.'" John 4:28 & 29

She was so ashamed by her sin that she waited to go to the well when no one else would see her. Yet here she is, proclaiming with confidence TO THE MEN of the city about a man WHO KNEW HER SINS! Not only was she free to be seen, she felt free enough to speak to the men, AND mention her source of shame. I would say something supernatural happened inside this woman! This was more than just a God-reconciliation, she was now reconciled with who she was and understood her God-design. All shame was gone, all guilt was gone, all fear was gone, all condemnation was gone, and she was free to be seen by the world.

The Bible goes on to tell us that the men of Samaria believed Jesus solely based on the testimony of the woman (John 4:39). I personally do not believe it was the testimony of just her words, but rather it was the testimony of her state of being. In other words, the evidence of Jesus was manifest through her actions. Her newfound boldness and confidence of His love despite her well-known sins spoke louder than her words.

The love of God changed her to the point where she was

compelled to do because of who she had become. The key was in her encounter at the well with Jesus; her ministry to others was the outcome. Her ministry started with her!

ON MISSION FOR CHRIST

The woman at the well was now on-mission. She discovered her God-assignment when Jesus broke through her wall with His love and it was that love that compelled her.

"For the love of Christ compels us, because we judge thus: that if One died for all, then all died; and He died for all, that those who live should live no longer for themselves, but for Him who died for them and rose again.

"Therefore, from now on, we regard no one according to the flesh. Even though we have known Christ according to the flesh, yet now we know Him thus no longer. Therefore, if anyone is in Christ, he is a new creation; old things have passed away; behold, all things have become new. Now all things are of God, who has reconciled us to Himself through Jesus Christ, and has given us the ministry of reconciliation, that is, that God was in Christ reconciling the world to Himself, not imputing their trespasses to them, and has committed to us the word of reconciliation.

"Now then, we are ambassadors for Christ, as though God were pleading through us: we implore you on Christ's behalf, be reconciled to God. For He made Him who knew no sin to be sin for us, that we might become the righteousness of God in Him."
2 Corinthians 5:14-21

We have discussed much through the first verses in this passage that speak of being reconciled to God and with self, but now we come to our ministry of reconciliation toward others. Read those last verses in *The Voice* translation...

"All of this is a gift from our Creator God, who has pursued us and brought us into a restored and healthy relationship with Him

through the Anointed. And He has given us the same mission, the ministry of reconciliation, to bring others back to Him. It is central to our good news that God was in the Anointed making things right between Himself and the world. This means He does not hold their sins against them. But it also means He charges us to proclaim the message that heals and restores our broken relationships with God and each other.

"So we are now representatives of the Anointed One, the Liberating King; God has given us a charge to carry through our lives—urging all people on behalf of the Anointed to become reconciled to the Creator God. He orchestrated this: the Anointed One, who had never experienced sin, became sin for us so that in Him we might embody the very righteousness of God." 2 Corinthians 5:18-21

We are called to represent God to those around us, to be ambassadors for Christ. This is a crucial part of our identity in Christ and the more we grow in God, the more our mission will grow in us! You see, we will not grow closer to God through our ministry to others, but rather we will grow closer to others through our ministry to God. Just like the woman at the well, our own reconciliation should drive our proclamations to the world. Unless we are reconciled vertically and internally, we will not be able to minister out of His love.

COMPELLED BY GOD

We see this compelling love throughout the Scriptures. In John 1, we see the trickling effect of two disciples who "followed Jesus." When Jesus asked them what they were seeking, they stated that they wanted to know where He was staying. To go beyond what they were seeking and fulfill their true need, the Bible says that Jesus did more than tell them where He was staying. He let them come and experience for themselves. In His desire to give them more than just knowledge, He afforded them an encounter, and they spent the day with Jesus! In turn, they went and told others and then brought them to Jesus (see John 1:35-42). Much like the woman at the well, their own experience with Jesus set a fire for ministry to others in their heart and they wanted the entire world to know.

The story right after that is similar in that Jesus found Phillip, connected with him, and then Phillip went and told Nathanial and brought Nathanial to meet Jesus. This is ministry at it finest, folks! It is simply the outcome of our own relationship with God. It is our own experience with Him and His love that should compel us to tell the world.

We see yet another example of this in the story of Peter and John in Acts 4.

"Now when they saw the boldness of Peter and John, and perceived that they were uneducated and untrained men, they marveled. And they realized that they had been with Jesus. And seeing the man who had been healed standing with them, they could say nothing against it. But when they had commanded them to go aside out of the council, they conferred among themselves, saying, 'What shall we do to these men? For, indeed, that a notable miracle has been done through them is evident to all who dwell in Jerusalem, and we cannot deny it. But so that it spreads no further among the people, let us severely threaten them, that from now on they speak to no man in this name.'

"So they called them and commanded them not to speak at all nor teach in the name of Jesus. But Peter and John answered and said to them, 'Whether it is right in the sight of God to listen to you more than to God, you judge. For we cannot but speak the things which we have seen and heard.'"

Need I say more? Our ministry to others should be an outcome of our own times of connection with God. If we are really sold on something, then we automatically want the world to know...so if we aren't compelled to go and minister Jesus with others, then it is possible that we might not be convinced ourselves...which is lack of God and self-reconciliation!

HIS GLORY, OUR COUNTENANCE

We are learning that our ministry to others should be compelled by His glory, which is released in us through our own relationship with God. Like Moses, because of his own personal intimacy with God, our faces should reflect God's radiance, meaning His glory (Exodus 34). Note that before Moses could move in his God-mission to the people, there was a lot of God and self-reconciling that took place!

The saturation of His love will cause His countenance to be seen in everything that you do.

"The Lord bless you and keep you;
The Lord make His face shine upon you,
And be gracious to you;
The Lord lift up His countenance upon you,
And give you peace."
Numbers 6:24-26

God will shine through who you are more than what you say or even how you act. In other words, your deeds can "look like" God, but if they are not compelled by God, then they will profit the kingdom nothing. This is what we call religion; acts compelled by duty.

God has created us to carry His light. Remember the lampstand that is in us? In order to keep your light ablaze and burning a pure flame, you must keep your wick trimmed and stay saturated in His holy oil. Then the Lord will "make His face shine upon you." God invites us to do what we can do, which is respond to His invitation of intimacy and connection with Him, and then He does what we can't do, makes our faces radiate His glory! In Greek this verse denotes the idea that the person of God (His glory) will be illuminated in us.

"You are the light of the world. A city that is set on a hill cannot be hidden. Nor do they light a lamp and put it under a basket, but on a lampstand, and it gives light to all who are in the house. Let your light so shine before men, that they may see your good works and

glorify your Father in heaven." Matthew 5:14-16

OUR MINISTRY OF JESUS

Jesus was the light of the world. Through Him, God's character and love was illuminated and made visible that all men would come to know the heart of the Father. Jesus was the arm of God reaching down from heaven to grab ahold of men and draw them into alignment with God. He was the Divine connect between God and man; hence man is reconciled to God THROUGH Jesus.

"For it pleased the Father that in Him all the fullness should dwell, and by Him to reconcile all things to Himself, by Him, whether things on earth or things in heaven, having made peace through the blood of His cross." Colossians 1:19-20

I love that this verse says that God was pleased with the assignment Jesus had been given. Just like Jesus, the priests' assignment was to provide a connection between God and man, and therefore, they also were given the "light of God" (the lampstand) to tend to. Now we, as the priesthood, also are carriers of His light. We bear the light of God in us via the Holy Spirit. And just as the priests and Jesus were assigned to connect man to God, so we also are assigned. This is our ministry of reconciliation. Now, hear me when I say we are not THE connect, only Jesus is the Divine connect. However, we must not diminish our ministry of being Jesus to the world. The veil that Moses wore to hide the fading of the glory of God on his own face is no longer necessary for those of us in Christ. This is because God's glory in us no longer fades; it doesn't come and go, in fact Scripture says it only grows more radiant as we walk by the Spirit.

"Therefore, since we have such hope, we use great boldness of speech—unlike Moses, who put a veil over his face so that the children of Israel could not look steadily at the end of what was passing away... Nevertheless when one turns to the Lord, the veil is taken away. Now the Lord is the Spirit; and where the Spirit of the

Lord is, there is liberty. But we all, with unveiled face, beholding as in a mirror the glory of the Lord, are being transformed into the same image from glory to glory, just as by the Spirit of the Lord."
2 Corinthians 3:12-13,16-18

There is an organic spiritual process that God is doing in each of our lives that will cause us to grow more into the image and likeness of Jesus on a daily basis, to allow us to be the evidence of God to the world. We have been assigned the ministry of Jesus. But remember, it wasn't so much about what Jesus did or what He said, rather it was His countenance of love that drew others to Him, and ultimately to God.

THE MINISTRY CYCLE

Let's bring this all home and take a look at how ministry should function in the kingdom. Take a look at this passage in Matthew.

"When the Son of Man comes in His glory, and all the holy angels with Him, then He will sit on the throne of His glory. All the nations will be gathered before Him, and He will separate them one from another, as a shepherd divides his sheep from the goats. And He will set the sheep on His right hand, but the goats on the left. Then the King will say to those on His right hand, 'Come, you blessed of My Father, inherit the kingdom prepared for you from the foundation of the world: for I was hungry and you gave Me food; I was thirsty and you gave Me drink; I was a stranger and you took Me in; I was naked and you clothed Me; I was sick and you visited Me; I was in prison and you came to Me.'

"Then the righteous will answer Him, saying, 'Lord, when did we see You hungry and feed You, or thirsty and give You drink? When did we see You a stranger and take You in, or naked and clothe You? Or when did we see You sick, or in prison, and come to You?' And the King will answer and say to them, 'Assuredly, I say to you, inasmuch as you did it to one of the least of these My brethren, you did it to Me.'" Matthew 25:31-40

Do you see it? Look at the full cycle that happens here. Our ministry to and reconciliation with God brings about self-reconciliation and self-ministry. From there, who we become compels a God mission of ministry to others...which ultimately is ministry to God! What a paradigm shift from what we are often taught. When ministry STARTS with God, in the end it glorifies God.

Read in this passage how, although we can plant and water the seed in the lives of others, only God can cause the seed of our ministry to grow. He brings the increase.

"I planted, Apollos watered, but God gave the increase. So neither he who plants is anything, nor he who waters, but God who gives the increase." 1 Corinthians 3:6-7

Read in this passage how any work that is not compelled and motivated by God will have a faulty foundation. Only ministry rooted in God will ultimately last and stand the test of time.

"For we are God's fellow workers; you are God's field, you are God's building. According to the grace of God which was given to me, as a wise master builder I have laid the foundation, and another builds on it. But let each one take heed how he builds on it. For no other foundation can anyone lay than that which is laid, which is Jesus Christ. Now if anyone builds on this foundation with gold, silver, precious stones, wood, hay, straw, each one's work will become clear; for the Day will declare it, because it will be revealed by fire; and the fire will test each one's work, of what sort it is. If anyone's work which he has built on it endures, he will receive a reward."
1 Corinthians 3:9-14

This is why it is so important that we start with God in anything that we do. Our works should flow from the heart of God. Recall Revelation 2 and the loss of the lampstand because the works of the church of Ephesus were no longer rooted in their first love. Stick to your first love and stay rooted in Him. This is what it means to *abide*, or *tarry and remain*, in Him. He is our sweet abode! Were it not for the Father's heart, we would not know love and would be ineffective in our ministry to others.

*"I am the vine, you are the branches. He who abides in Me, and I in him, bears much fruit; for without Me you can do nothing...By this **my Father is glorified,** that you bear much fruit; so you will be My disciples. **As the Father loves Me, I also have loved you; abide in My love.**" John 15:5,8-9 (Emphasis mine)*

Even Jesus understood the importance of abiding in the Father's love by being loved by Him first. It was out of His own saturation of the Father's glory that He was able to love us. Ultimately, the Father was glorified through the love that Jesus manifested to us on behalf of the Father. All so we would be reconciled with God.

This love cycle, the cycle of loving and being loved, was established from the foundations of the earth

PRAYER PRACTICE

Father, I thank You for drawing me into Your sweet abode. Thank You that I find answers in Your presence and that Your presence and love in me bears much fruit. I thank You for teaching me how to stay rooted in You and for the productivity Your love brings through me. I pray that I would understand the design for Your love cycle and how it affects every interaction I have and ultimately how I will connect with others. May I have more than just knowledge, but may I walk in the wisdom of this knowledge and may I freely love and be loved all the days of my life.

In Jesus' name I pray, Amen.

Chapter 19
Reconciling with Others

Although we have pretty much come to the end of this book, I would be remiss if I did not circle back to the very first section on relationships and the practical challenges they can bring. We have talked in regards to loving others and ministering reconciliation to others. But there is a difference between ministering the reconciliation of God to people and actually walking in reconciliation with people. Just like it is possible to be reconciled with God, yet not with ourselves, it also is possible to be reconciled with God and self, yet have unreconciled relationships.

Let's be honest, it is somewhat easy to love those whom we don't necessarily have daily connection with or who are not a part of our inner circle. Not minding doesn't really matter when it comes to dealing with those who don't really have an effect on you. Ministering to those outside of our circle can be more easily viewed as an assignment, which lessens the potential for personal hurts or wounds. My purpose is to empower you, not just in kingdom relationships, but also in your regular daily connections; your close friends, your co-workers, your family, and your spouses. So how do you grasp this kingdom-mindset even with those you are connected with through the soul?

While I could write for another one hundred pages breaking down the nuts and bolts of challenges we face within relationships, I believe the answer still lies in understanding your God-design and your assignment within relationships, ESPECIALLY to those in your inner circle. Although we don't want our close relationships to function as simply an assignment, they still are. You get the perks of connection, fellowship, joy, friendship, and love, but to forget the spirit assignments will cause you to lose your focus and the relationship will no longer be about God, only about you and/or the other party. Part of the beauty of these relationships is that your soul is satisfied and filled with joy, however, God must remain the point. That fact that you get personal pleasures is the overflow of God, but at the root, even your closest relationships should still be all about glorifying God.

RECONCILIATION IN YOU

I have given multiple examples of relationship challenges throughout this book, but let it be clearly said, reconciling with others starts with you. This is why focusing on God and you first is so important. As I mentioned earlier, many people come for counseling because of the challenges within their relationships. However, we typically end up spending the majority of our sessions working through their own reconciliation with God and themselves. This is at the heart of reconciling with others. It is amazing how this process organically works out the kinks around you. When your inward perspective for God and yourself shifts, your outward perspective toward others will shift as well.

As you reconcile with God and self, you gain God's heart for others. You are able to see them, not from a personal perspective, but from a kingdom perspective, even when it really is personal. This is why we are exhorted to pray for those who hurt us and offend us. It is not because what they did or their offense is OK. Praying for them gives you a God-view of them and softens your heart so that although their act may not be OK, you are OK, even in their offense. You see, walking in His design for you will guard you in every relationship. It really isn't about how you are treated or any offense, it is about how you respond and who you are in the midst of it.

Remember the story of Jesus and His inner circle, and how they fell asleep on Him during His greater hour of need?

"Then Jesus came with them to a place called Gethsemane, and said to the disciples, 'Sit here while I go and pray over there.' And He took with Him Peter and the two sons of Zebedee, and He began to be

sorrowful and deeply distressed. Then He said to them, 'My soul is exceedingly sorrowful, even to death. Stay here and watch with Me.'

"He went a little farther and fell on His face, and prayed, saying, 'O My Father, if it is possible, let this cup pass from Me; nevertheless, not as I will, but as You will.'

"Then He came to the disciples and found them sleeping, and said to Peter, 'What! Could you not watch with Me one hour? Watch and pray, lest you enter into temptation. The spirit indeed is willing, but the flesh is weak.'

"Again, a second time, He went away and prayed, saying, 'O My Father, if this cup cannot pass away from Me unless I drink it, Your will be done.' And He came and found them asleep again, for their eyes were heavy.

"So He left them, went away again, and prayed the third time, saying the same words. Then He came to His disciples and said to them, 'Are you still sleeping and resting? Behold, the hour is at hand, and the Son of Man is being betrayed into the hands of sinners. Rise, let us be going. See, My betrayer is at hand.'"
Matthew 26:36-46

I love this story because although Jesus was clearly let down by the apathy and seemingly lack of concern of His friends, He remained faithful to them. His character was unwavering and His love for them was unconditional. He was more concerned with His assignment of loving them than He was their weakness in being there for Him. He had no time to be offended and He could not be distracted by anything personal. He was focused on fulfilling His design and purpose. This was the glory of God in Him.

RECONCILIATION BRINGS PEACE

It is important to note that reconciliation does not always look like the relationship necessarily being restored. It does not mean that you are back to being buddy-buddy or even friends again. You can be reconciled, yet not be in relationship, conversely, you can be in relationship, yet not be reconciled. Remember, reconciliation starts in you, which means reconciliation is more about your heart and attitude. So we must do all we can do to pursue health and connection with others, but ultimately, our goal is to be reconciled with God and within ourselves in regard to every relationship. This is the hope and power that we have even in the midst of what seems like hopeless and powerless situations.

"If it is possible, as much as depends on you, live peaceably with all men." Romans 12:18

This verse reminds us that we can only do what WE can do, meaning we can't control how the other party might or might not respond. My only goal is to walk in the heart of God. In doing so, I AM successful, regardless of the outcome I see. Simply said, reconciliation with others is being at peace in your heart in regard to that person or situation. This is why it is possible to reconcile with someone who is deceased. God will always honor us as we walk in obedience to His design for relationships. We can extend grace, peace, and love to others, regardless of how they respond or their ability to respond.

"When wisdom enters your heart,
And knowledge is pleasant to your soul,
Discretion will preserve you;
Understanding will keep you,
To deliver you from the way of evil,
From the man who speaks perverse things." Proverbs 2:10-12

"And your righteousness shall go before you;
The glory of the Lord shall be your rear guard." Isaiah 58:8b

Obedience to His character ultimately keeps you and guards your heart from the turmoil of conflict. This goes back to mirroring His spirit and not the spirits of man. Abiding in His heart and responding the way He would will cause you to love one another as He has loved you.

*This is my commandment, that you love one another **as I have loved you**." John 15:12 (Emphasis mine)*

God's love for you is the most powerful force in your life. Any conflicts and challenges that you face with people and in your relationships may FEEL overwhelming and threaten to take over your life, but nothing or no one trumps God. This Truth will keep you from reacting out of the flesh and will keep you focused on God and how He is growing your design through all things.

"And we know that all things work together for good to those who love God, to those who are the called according to His purpose." Romans 8:28

His purpose is to grow you into your image of Jesus. Every challenge, every conflict, every wound, every spot of anger, no matter the relationship, is an opportunity to increase in your likeness of Him. He is not willing to leave you immature or incomplete. He is working all things for your good and His glory. This is why we can consider any trial or tribulation, which OFTEN come through relationships, a joy.

"My brethren, count it all joy when you fall into various trials, knowing that the testing of your faith produces patience. But let patience have its perfect work, that you may be perfect and complete, lacking nothing. If any of you lacks wisdom, let him ask of God, who gives to all liberally and without reproach, and it will be given to him." James 1:2-5

This verse also reminds us that our wisdom is found in God; and we often need wisdom when dealing with others. He will guide you in every relationship and will not just give you wisdom; He will give it to you generously and without finding any fault. This is a promise you can stand on, that in your time of need, He will be your guiding light that will illuminate the path of righteousness in every relationship.

SACRIFICING FOR GOD

Sometimes pursuing reconciliation means pressing in and being willing to lay aside your feelings and thoughts, while other times it means setting healthy boundaries. Either way it is about learning how to enforce God's design in your own life while desiring the same for the other party involved. Again, it is not about you, nor about the other person, but about glorifying God.

"Greater love has no one than this, than to lay down one's life for his friends." John 15:13

Jesus ultimately demonstrated the perfect balance of sacrifice without sacrificing His design. In fact, His sacrifice actually fulfilled His design. This is because His sacrifice wasn't really for man; it was for God. If God compels everything you do, then any sacrifice you make is never for any one person, it is for God. This is how you ensure that your sacrifice is neither about you nor the other person, but only about God. Again, the result is in God's glorification and not man's!

God's heart is that your relationships reflect the perfection of His love. This is a part of your ministry to God. Just as the connection Jesus had with man inspired others to connect with God, so your relationships should inspire people to connect with Him as well. This is only possible as you grow in security in His love and confidence in His design for you and for relationships. It is when you are free to love and to be loved just the way you are!

PRAYER PRACTICE

God, I thank You that You are my role model. You are my example and my inspiration of what it looks like to reconcile with others. You stopped at nothing to reconcile with me and I pray that my heart would reflect that. May I mirror You in all things and seek You for wisdom in every relationship. And may Your love compel me

to love as You did. Keep my heart at peace with You, Lord, even when things around me are not at peace. Relationships are not easy, and I don't always feel love and kindness, but I trust You to continue to grow me as I choose to walk in Your ways!

In Jesus' name I pray, Amen.

Conclusion

I included Section 1 in this book to empower and equip you, as you move forward in your pursuit of healthy relationships. It is the nuts and bolts of working out your relationships with others. Your goal is to establish healthy relationships with others, but the key lies in your relationship with God and you. As I stated in the introduction, one section without the other would be incomplete. I highly recommend that upon completing this conclusion, you flip back to the front of this book and reread the first section. I think you might be surprised how much more it will resonate after reading Section 2.

In conclusion, I want to remind you of the story of Job. Job was a man who was pleasing to God and walked in His ways.

"There was a man in the land of Uz, whose name was Job; and that man was blameless and upright, and one who feared God and shunned evil." Job 1:1

As a result, Job was prosperous and lived a life of abundance. However, the Lord allowed Satan to test him through illness, deaths, and an overall loss of all that he once owned and possessed. We don't really know why, but I believe that God was refining fear and religion in Job. Scripture mentions that Job daily offered sacrifices on behalf of his children, "just in case" their hearts were not right with God.

"So it was, when the days of feasting had run their course, that Job would send and sanctify them, and he would rise early in the morning and offer burnt offerings according to the number of them

all. For Job said, 'It may be that my sons have sinned and cursed God in their hearts.' Thus Job did regularly." Job 1:5

Again, I can only speculate, but what we do know is that God allows trials for the purpose of growing us and reconciling things that are not in line with His heart. So, I think it is fair to conclude that this was the case for Job. There were things in his heart that God wanted to work out, thus reconciling ALL things.

The majority of the book is all about Job reconciling with God why tribulation has come into His life. He wrestles with God, trying to reconcile what He knows about God through what he has experienced. If that wasn't hard enough, he had many relationships in his life that were less than encouraging; namely his wife and three close friends. His wife suggests that Job "curse God and die" (Job 2:9), no doubt stirring up Job's questions about who God is and why He allowed this. His three friends, on the other hand, suggest that Job had sin in His life. While his wife questions the integrity of God and His character, his friends question Job's integrity and his character. Needless to say, none of them were helpful and encouraging in his time of need. The whole book is basically a book of questions; his wife asking him questions, his friends asking him questions, Job asking them questions, Job asking God questions...and then at the end, God asking Job questions. There is serious reasoning and reconciling taking place through the whole book. Then, after 41 chapters of this, we see Job finally come to a conclusion and repent .

"Then Job answered the Lord and said:
'I know that You can do everything,
And that no purpose of Yours can be withheld from You.
You asked, 'Who is this who hides counsel without knowledge?'
Therefore I have uttered what I did not understand,
Things too wonderful for me, which I did not know.
Listen, please, and let me speak;
You said, 'I will question you, and you shall answer Me.'
'I have heard of You by the hearing of the ear,
But now my eye sees You.

Therefore I abhor myself,
And repent in dust and ashes.'"
Job 42:1-6

You see through this passage the shift where Job recognizes that what he once only believed in his head, he now believes in his heart. This is the shift we see when someone is not just reconciled with God, but they are also reconciled within themselves. Job was fully reconciled and came to the conclusion that he really did serve God with a pure heart; solely because of who God was and not for just what He gave. Thus, his fear of losing everything and having to operate in religious duty was sifted out of him.

But what happens next is fascinating. God calls Job to intercede and pray for his friends. You remember, those friends who were less than encouraging and bashed Job's character throughout the majority of the book? I don't know about you, but I would have been irritated and angry. And it is possible that Job was, too. However, Job's reconciliation with God and himself caused him to surrender. He knew that reconciliation with his friends was not really about them, it was about God and His design for them...and for Job. So Job prays for them, and it was the prayers for his friends that brought about his restoration.

"And the Lord restored Job's losses when he prayed for his friends. Indeed the Lord gave Job twice as much as he had before." Job 42:10

I believe that Job's personal healing came when he reconciled with God and within himself, but I believe he was restored when he prayed for his friends. We can be sure that Job's complete reconciliation is what loosened the paradise of God.

This is God's desire for all of us; that we reconcile all things with Him, ourselves, and those around us, thus walking in His paradise all the days of our lives.

It is my prayer that through this book, every aspect of who YOU are is reconciled with God and that you reconcile His design for you in your own heart as well. In short, I pray that YOU are healed. Although this book addresses relationships, the purpose is for you to understand who YOU are and your need to love and to be loved. It is only as you come into freedom with God and freedom within yourself that you will experience freedom in your relationships, thus connecting at a deeper, healthier level and ultimately establishing healthy relationships.

PRAYER PRACTICE

Wow, God! You have done such an incredible work in my life and in the life of my relationships. I thank You for teaching me the importance of not just loving others, but also of being loved. What a gift it is to be able to connect without fear and what satisfaction it brings to my soul. I pray that Your love may be seen in every relationship that I have and that I am always rooted in Your character. Teach me to abide in You as You abide in me. Make me ever-aware of every opportunity to glorify You in every interaction.

Finally, I pray that just as You rescue me, I pray that others are rescued as well. I pray I will know the depths of Your love for them and the value they bring to Your kingdom. Show them their worth and their design for love. Fill them with courage to love and to be loved more freely. I bind up any fear and speak boldly that where the Spirit of the Lord is, there is liberty!

In Jesus' name I pray, Amen.

About Crazy8 Ministries

Mission: A ministry compelled by the love of Christ to reach and come alongside others and bring wholeness to the body, soul, and spirit; healing for yesterday, help in today, victory in tomorrow.
Attacking poverty one person at a time.

Crazy8 Ministries was founded in 2011 and started as a conference ministry where founder, Lisa Schwarz, designed and developed conferences and travelled around the United States preaching and teaching the gospel in many arenas. It was her desire to offer more than just a "weekend experience." With people contacting her in need of further ministry, the ministry evolved into what is now the Crazy8 Ministries facility, located in Johnson County, Texas. Because each person is at a different place in the healing process of living out the fullness of the gospel, there are several different arms of the ministry. Each arm helps to accomplish the mission through its own unique focus and partner together with one heart and one mind for one purpose: to meet the needs of each person that is served. The goal is to bring those served into the wholeness of Jesus Christ and move them into a place of thriving, body, soul, and spirit.

The Housing Program offers a long term home for individuals and families who are in a "sick circumstance" and offer the hope, help and freedom of

Jesus Christ in a practical way through a loving, secure, multi-family home. The program is an 18-24 month restorative program that is designed to come alongside to provide emotional, spiritual, and physical help in their today, meeting them right where they are.

The Biblical Counseling/Discipleship Ministry (BCDM) focuses on ministering to those who suffer from "sick thinking or sick emotions" through one-on-one free counseling and discipleship as well as group opportunities. The BCDM comes alongside others in order to instill hope, healing, and life transformation through the power of the Holy Spirit and the Word of God, so they may live victoriously in Jesus Christ.

The Outreach Ministry focuses on serving and providing opportunities within our community in order to build relationships and touch others with the love of Christ and the transforming power of the gospel; working toward city transformation by promoting unity and oneness of heart, to proclaim that we are a city of one King.

Crazy8 Ministries founded the City on a Hill Festival held in Burleson, TX. This annual event is a day of free family fun that spotlights the collaboration of services & opportunities working together as the body of Christ in order to transform their community into a 'City on a Hill'. It has grown to serve over 5,000 patrons each year.

To learn more about Crazy8 Ministries, visit www.crazy8ministries.com.

About the Author

Lisa Schwarz is a nationally recognized speaker, bestselling author, Certified Biblical Counselor, Professional Life Coach, Brain Health Coach, and Founder/CEO of Crazy8 Ministries.

A premier event planner, Lisa delivers her impactful message nationwide at conferences, workshops, and home experiences. Enforcing purpose: maximizing who you are, what you do and cultures around you is the passion that drives her. Lisa is uniquely experienced as a disciple-maker to individuals, mentor to groups and expert leader for developing restorative housing programs.

Equipping and empowering others to experience transformation through Jesus Christ guides her purpose for *community* and belief in the power of unity; *together we are better.* Lisa is available for sharing her experience, education and expertise with others engaged with improving life for other people.

She and her husband, Brad, reside in Texas, and have 6 children, a daughter and son-in-law, and 2 grandchildren.

Also By Lisa Schwarz

Enforcing You: Activating Your Kingdom Identity in Christ
ISBN: 978-1-7340693-4-1

Enforcing Purpose: Discovering God's Calling to Maximize Your Future
ISBN: 978-1-7340693-5-8

Enforcing Prayer: Biblical Declarations for Your Daily Devotions
ISBN: 978-1-7340693-3-4

Mastering Your Seasons
ISBN: 978-1-7340693-9-6

Come and See: The Jesus Approach to Equipping Biblical Disciples
ISBN: 978-1-7340693-7-2

The Pursuit of His Glory: Seeking the Character of God
ISBN: 978-1-7340693-6-5

'

Made in the USA
Columbia, SC
05 May 2025

57460997R00126